S. Hrg. 113–549

RUSSIA AND DEVELOPMENTS IN UKRAINE

HEARING

BEFORE THE

COMMITTEE ON FOREIGN RELATIONS
UNITED STATES SENATE

ONE HUNDRED THIRTEENTH CONGRESS

SECOND SESSION

JULY 9, 2014

Printed for the use of the Committee on Foreign Relations

Available via the World Wide Web: http://www.gpo.gov/fdsys/

U.S. GOVERNMENT PUBLISHING OFFICE

WASHINGTON : 2015

93–035 PDF

(II)

CONTENTS

(III)

RUSSIA AND DEVELOPMENTS IN UKRAINE

WEDNESDAY, JULY 9, 2014

U.S. SENATE,
COMMITTEE ON FOREIGN RELATIONS,
Washington, DC.

The committee met, pursuant to notice, at 9:45 a.m., in room SD–419, Dirksen Senate Office Building, Hon. Robert Menendez (chairman of the committee) presiding.

Present: Senators Menendez, Shaheen, Murphy, Kaine, Markey, Corker, Rubio, Johnson, Flake, and Barrasso.

OPENING STATEMENT OF HON. ROBERT MENENDEZ, U.S. SENATOR FROM NEW JERSEY

The CHAIRMAN. This hearing will come to order.

We have two distinguished panels today to help us look more closely at developments in the Ukraine. We are pleased to have on our first panel the Assistant Secretaries from State, Treasury, and Defense to brief us on the situation on the ground, and on our second panel, two former National Security Advisors to provide insights into the broader geopolitical implications of Putin's actions in Ukraine.

In the past week, Ukraine appears to have mobilized around its new President. Ukrainian Armed Forces have been actively re-closing their border with Russia and pushing back Russian separatists. At the same time, President Putin's instigation of this conflict continues to breed uncertainty as to whether a corner has, in fact, been turned. In my view, President Putin is entirely capable of trying to divide Ukraine one day and then, when the international community applies pressure, withdraw from the scene long enough to avoid the international community's scrutiny, while effectively continuing his aggression to achieve his intended goal.

In June I wrote to President Obama, asking him to seriously consider implementing additional targeted sanctions as soon as possible to deter Putin from further destabilizing Ukraine. I fully appreciate the importance of acting in concert with our European allies to ensure that sanctions have their intended effect, but, at the same time, we should not hesitate to act unilaterally to support an independent Ukraine and counter malign Russian interference when delay threatens these goals, our strategic objectives, or our national interests. In the long run, a stable and secure region will serve our national interests and enhance opportunities for U.S. and European businesses.

In my view, unless Putin is confronted with strong disincentives, he will continue to ensure that the Ukrainian Government will not be able to stabilize the situation and he will position himself to fill the power vacuum when the government cannot fulfill the needs of parts of the Ukrainian people.

A question for our panelists today is, What steps and measures must Putin take now to demonstrate his commitment to resolving the conflict? And at what point would you call his bluff and proceed with additional sanctions?

We are pleased to have distinguished panelists before the committee. We look forward to gaining a deeper insight into what is happening on the ground, as well as the broader geopolitical ramifications of Russia's actions.

With that, let me turn to Senator Corker, the ranking member, for his comments.

OPENING STATEMENT OF HON. BOB CORKER, U.S. SENATOR FROM TENNESSEE

Senator CORKER. Thank you, Mr. Chairman, and thanks for calling the hearing.

I welcome our witnesses on both panels. I think we have got an outstanding group of people here today that I know will be very informative.

I know this is almost becoming a cliche, but Russia seems to be a master at escalating and de-escalating at the same time, acts of duplicity which keep the Western world off balance. So, I look forward to hearing from our witnesses today at what phase they think we are in relative to Russia.

We have some people here that are very committed public servants that I respect, but, I have to say, sometimes I am embarrassed for you as you constantly talk about sanctions, and yet we never see them put in place. So, I hope you will enlighten us today as to where we might be in that regard. Media outlets have talked about another round of sanctions that you are preparing. I hope that you will illuminate those today and talk to us a little bit about, as the chairman mentioned, what needs to occur, from Russia's standpoint, to either cause those to be put in place or not put in place.

But, again, I really feel like the sanctions threats have been very hollow; candidly, they have some of the same characteristics of the redline we talked about in Syria. I certainly hope that changes soon, because, in getting to my final point, I worry that where we are going with Russia, relative to Ukraine, is what a National Security Advisor in Eastern Europe said to me recently; that he fears that our policy is taking us to a place where we are going to have a bitter peace with Russia, where, in essence, we sweep under the rug the actions that have taken place in Crimea and continue to take place in eastern Ukraine and we, basically, get back to business as usual. It looks like that is where we may be heading, which, over time, could lead to some more major consequences in Eastern Europe and the world. I hope that is not the policy that this administration is embarking on.

I thank the witnesses for being here today, and look forward to your testimony.

The CHAIRMAN. Thank you, Senator Corker.

For our first panel today, we welcome back Assistant Secretary of State for European and Eurasian Affairs, Victoria Nuland; Daniel Glaser, who is the Assistant Secretary of Treasury for Terrorist Financing; and Derek Chollet, who is the Assistant Secretary of Defense for International Security Affairs.

Let me remind our panelists that your full statements will be included in the record. I would ask you to try to summarize them in 5 minutes so we can enter into a dialogue.

In the course of just receiving your testimony, Madam Secretary, I skimmed through it, and I hope that you will be ready to respond, if not in your statement, then when we get to Q&A, to this one line on the third page, where it says, ''we are ready to impose more costs, including targeted sector-specific sanctions, very soon if Russia does not decidedly change course and break its ties with separatists.'' It seems like we have heard that, ''very soon'' before. So, maybe you can quantify that for us.

And, with that, we recognize you.

STATEMENT OF HON. VICTORIA NULAND, ASSISTANT SECRETARY OF STATE FOR EUROPEAN AND EURASIAN AFFAIRS, U.S. DEPARTMENT OF STATE, WASHINGTON, DC

Ms. NULAND. Thank you, Chairman Menendez, Ranking Member Corker, and members of this committee, and thank you for the opportunity to speak with you again today on the situation in Ukraine.

As you said, longer statement will be submitted for the record.

In previous testimony before this committee, I have outlined four pillars of United States policy: support for Ukraine as it tackles its urgent political, economic, and security challenges; diplomatic efforts to try to de-escalate the crisis; imposing further costs, including targeted sectoral sanctions, on Russia and separatists who are fomenting violence and unrest in Ukraine; and, number four, reassurance of frontline NATO allies and friends, like Georgia and Moldova.

Today, in my statement, I will focus on the first two lines of effort. Assistant Secretary Chollet will talk about our security support for Ukraine and our allies. And Assistant Secretary Glaser will talk about sanctions policy. But, of course, we will all answer your questions.

Since I last appeared before you, voters from across Ukraine took to the polls on May 25 and elected President Poroshenko with 54.7 percent of the vote. Just weeks and days earlier, many doubted that the elections would even take place. It was the determination and courage of millions of Ukrainians to choose their own future that made free, fair elections possible along with the support of the international community. But, as you know, Ukraine's security remains under threat as fighting continues in eastern parts of the country, and Crimea remains under occupation.

Against this backdrop, the United States is supporting Ukraine in this hour of its need. We have stepped up our security assistance, which Assistant Secretary Chollet will discuss. However, the more lasting antidote to separatism and outside interference, over the medium term, is for Ukraine to succeed as a democratic, free-market state, and to beat back the corruption, dependence, and external pressure that have thwarted Ukrainians' aspirations for decades.

Since the onset of this crisis, with this Congress' support, we have provided Ukraine with a billion-dollar loan guarantee specifically targeted to soften the impact of economic reforms on the country's most vulnerable. We are also providing approximately $196 million in other assistance to Ukraine this year. Of this, we have already authorized $75 million in support of economic reform, anticorruption measures, nonpartisan electoral assistance, nonlethal security assistance, and humanitarian aid for Ukrainians internally displaced from Crimea and eastern Ukraine. We are now working with President Poroshenko, Prime Minister Yatsenyuk, and their team to direct the remaining $59 million in four key areas: first, support for economic growth and reform; second, countering corruption; third, energy diversification and efficiency; and, four, constitutional reform and national unity. We will be sending up a formal congressional notification very shortly, but let me just give you some highlights.

In the area of economic reform and growth, we will complement World Bank and IMF programs by working to help strengthen the Ukrainian banking sector, making the business climate more competitive and attractive to investors, and helping Ukraine diversify its export markets.

Our anticorruption support will help support the government's new 3-year program and bolster its ability to deter, to detect, investigate, and prosecute corruption wherever it festers, and support civil society, the media, business, and government as they work together to root it out.

In the energy area, we will help the government to restructure the sector and to deploy new technologies to increase energy yields and efficiency, and to assist Ukraine in developing national plans for sustainable use of natural resources.

And finally, we will help the government implement the constitutional reform and broad decentralization of power at the local and regional level that has been central to President Poroshenko's peace plan and to rebuilding national unity.

As we support Ukraine economically, as you know, we have also worked in lockstep with the Ukrainian Government and our European allies and partners to try to de-escalate the tensions with Russia and with Russian-backed separatists through repeated rounds of diplomacy, which we have talked about here. In successive settings, we have supported the Ukrainian Government's offers to address those concerns that are legitimate, of eastern Ukrainians and Russian speakers, by political means, and to offer an off-ramp to separatists and to their Russian backers. These efforts have culminated most recently in President Poroshenko's broad-reaching peace plan, which he first presented in his inaugural address, which offers amnesty to separatists who lay down their arms, political dialogue, broad decentralization of power—in short, virtually all of the things that the separatists and their backers in Moscow have said that are needed.

President Poroshenko, as you know, also initiated, on June 27, a 10-day unilateral cease-fire to try to provide space for dialogue with separatists. But, as you also know, this cease-fire was met with 10 days of violence, bloodshed, and separatists land-grabs as Russia simultaneously allowed tanks, heavy artillery, and fighters to flow across the border.

On June 27, EU leaders again called on Russia to end all support for separatists, to control the border, to use its influence with separatists to return the three border checkpoints to Ukrainian authorities that they had taken, to release hostages, and to launch substantial negotiations on the peace plan. These are the same criteria that the United States is continuing to use to measure Russia's willingness to de-escalate tension in Ukraine. As President Obama has said, "We will judge Russia by its actions, not by its words."

The United States and Europe have imposed repeated rounds of sanctions to increase the cost Russia pays for its choices. And, as you quoted, Mr. Chairman, we are ready to impose more costs, including targeted sector-specific sanctions, very soon if Russia does not decisively change course and break its support for separatists.

As Russia's economy teeters on the bring of recession, in part from the cost of its intervention in Ukraine and the impact of our sanctions, as noted in the latest IMF report released a week ago, Russians need to ask themselves what their government's policy has really delivered for them or for the people of Ukraine, other than economic hardship, violence, kidnapping, and death.

Today, in Slovyansk, in Kramatorsk, and in other towns recently retaken by Ukrainian forces from the separatists, the Ukrainian Government is delivering humanitarian aid and restoring services. They are also working to restore the Ukrainian people's faith in their government's ability to provide a better future. Ukraine's success or failure in its struggle for peace, reconciliation, and human dignity will impact the future of the entire region, and, with it, the prospect for achieving America's 20-year objective of a Europe whole, free, and at peace.

We, therefore, continue to have profound national interests in supporting the people of Ukraine in their quest for a more stable, democratic, and prosperous future. And, in this effort, we deeply appreciate Congress' continued bipartisan support.

We look forward to your questions.

[The prepared statement of Ms. Nuland follows:]

PREPARED STATEMENT OF VICTORIA NOLAND

Chairman Menendez, Ranking Member Corker and members of this committee, thank you for the opportunity to speak to you today on the situation in Ukraine and for your personal investment in the country's future. As many of you know from your travels, Ukrainians deeply appreciate this committee's bipartisan engagement on behalf of their country's security, democracy, and sovereignty.

In previous testimony before this committee, I have outlined four pillars of U.S. policy: support for Ukraine as it tackles urgent political, economic, and security challenges; diplomatic efforts to de-escalate the crisis and to encourage Russia to end support for separatists; readiness to impose further costs—including targeted sectoral sanctions—on Russia and separatists for fomenting violence and unrest in Ukraine; and reassurance of frontline NATO allies and friends like Georgia and Moldova. Today, I will focus on the first two lines of effort. A/S Chollet will talk about our security support for Ukraine and our NATO and partner reassurance measures. A/S Glaser will discuss sanctions policy.

Since I last appeared before you, voters from across Ukraine took to the polls on May 25 and elected President Poroshenko with 54.7 percent of the vote. Just weeks and days earlier, many doubted the elections would take place, let alone result in such a strong democratic mandate for change. It was the determination and courage of millions of Ukrainians to choose their own future that made free, fair elections possible, along with the steadfast support of the international community, including intensive electoral monitoring. In the weeks since, President Poroshenko has launched a 15-point peace plan, reached out to the east with offers of dialogue and reconciliation, and signed the final economic chapters of Ukraine's historic Association Agreement/Deep and Comprehensive Free Trade Area with the European Union. But Ukraine's security remains under threat: despite regaining control of Slovyansk and Kramotorsk, fierce fighting continues to rage in parts of eastern Ukraine; heavy weapons, materiel and support have flown across the Russian border; Russia has thousand troops deployed on Ukraine's eastern border, and Crimea remains under occupation.

Against this backdrop, the United States is supporting Ukraine in its hour of need. We have stepped up our security assistance, which A/S Chollet will discuss. However, the most lasting antidote to separatism and outside interference over the medium term is for Ukraine to succeed as a democratic, free market state, and to beat back the corruption, dependence, and external pressure that have thwarted Ukrainians' aspirations for decades. Since the onset of the crisis, with your support, we have provided Ukraine with a $1 billion loan guarantee specifically targeted to soften the impact of economic reforms on the country's most vulnerable. We are also providing approximately $196 million in other assistance to Ukraine this year. Of this, we have already authorized nearly $75 million in support for economic reforms and anticorruption measures; nonpartisan electoral assistance including the OSCE's special monitoring mission and other election observers; nonlethal security assistance; and humanitarian aid for Ukrainians internally displaced from Crimea or the East.

We are now working with President Poroshenko, Prime Minister Yatsenyuk, and their team to direct $59 million to efforts in four target areas: support for economic growth and reform; countercorruption; energy diversification and efficiency; and constitutional reform and national unity. We will send up a congressional notification very shortly, but let me share some highlights.

In the area of economic reform and growth, we will complement World Bank and IMF-led fiscal and financial sector reforms with programs to strengthen the banking sector; to make the business climate more competitive and attractive to investors, including in the agriculture sector; and to help Ukraine diversify its export markets. We are also looking at how we can support President Poroshenko's plan for economic revitalization of the country's east and south.

Our anticorruption support will help the government implement its recently announced 3-year anticorruption strategy and 6-month action plan by bolstering Ukraine's ability to deter, detect, investigate and prosecute corruption wherever it festers; and by supporting citizens, civil society, media, business and the government as they work together to confront this scourge.

U.S. support in the energy area will include expertise and advice to the government as it seeks to restructure and reform the sector, and deploy new technologies to increase energy yields and promote efficiency. And we will assist Ukraine in developing national plans for sustainable use and management of natural resources.

And we will help the government with the constitutional reform and broad decentralization of power that President Poroshenko has pledged as an integral part of his peace plan and his effort to rebuild national unity. This will include support and advice at the federal, regional, and local level to implement political reform and decentralization, and support for free and fair parliamentary elections when they are called.

As we support Ukraine economically, we have also worked in lock-step with the Ukrainian Government and our European allies and partners to try to de-escalate tensions with Russia and Russian-backed separatists. In successive settings, from Secretary Kerry's bilateral meetings with Russian Foreign Minister Lavrov in March to the April 17th Geneva Joint Statement of U.S.-Ukrainian-Russian and EU Foreign Ministers to the June 5th G7 declaration, we have supported the Ukrainian Government's offers to address the legitimate concerns of eastern Ukrainians and Russian speakers by political means, and to offer an off-ramp to separatists and their Russian backers. These efforts culminated in President Poroshenko's peace plan, which offers amnesty to separatists who lay down their arms, political dialogue, broad decentralization of power to Ukraine's regions and localities—including over finances, language and culture, and local elections—in short, virtually all the things that the separatists and Moscow had demanded for months. President Poroshenko also initiated a 10-day unilateral cease-fire from June 20–30 to provide the space for dialogue with the separatists. But as you know, the cease-fire was instead met with 10 days of violence, bloodshed, and land grabs by Russian-backed separatists. Three Ukrainian border posts fell into their hands during this period.

Russia allowed tanks, heavy artillery, and fighters to flow across the border, and continued to build up its forces and weapons on Ukraine's border.

On June 27, EU leaders again called on Russia to end all support for separatists; to control the border; to help establish an effective OSCE monitoring regime; and use its influence with separatists to return the three border checkpoints to Ukrainian authorities, release the hostages they hold and launch substantial negotiations on the implementation of President Poroshenko's peace plan. These are the same criteria that the U.S. will continue to use to measure Russia's willingness to de-escalate tensions in Ukraine. As the President has said, we will judge Russia by its actions, not its words. Russia has made too many commitments at the diplomatic table over the past 4 months that have been rendered hollow by the weapons, cash, and fighters that continue to flow across the border to fuel the fight in eastern Ukraine. In response, the U.S. and Europe have imposed repeated rounds of sanctions to increase the cost Russia pays for its choices. And we are ready to impose more costs—including targeted sector-specific sanctions—very soon if Russia does not decisively change course and break its ties with separatists.

As Russia's economy teeters on the brink of recession in part from the cost of its intervention in Ukraine and the impact of U.S. and international sanctions as noted in last week's IMF report, Russians need to ask themselves what their government's policy has really delivered for them or the people of Ukraine except economic hardship, violence, kidnapping, and death. In Crimea, inflation has risen to 16.8 percent, tourism down 35 percent, and exports are plummeting. In Donetsk and Luhansk, separatists have engaged in looting and bank robbery, prevented the payment of pensions and wages, and held much of the civilian population hostage in their homes. Now that separatists are on the run, their tactics have become even more brutal as they set up landmines and roadside bombs and destroy bridges and other critical infrastructure.

Today, in Slovyansk, Kramatorsk and the surrounding towns that Ukrainian forces have recently taken back from separatists' control, the government is focused on delivering humanitarian aid, water, food and supplies and reestablishing services from railway service to pension payments. They are working to restore Ukrainian citizens' faith in their democracy, their govenunent and its ability to serve people who have been abused for too long.

Ukraine's success or failure in its struggle for peace, reconciliation, and human dignity will impact the future of the whole region, and with it, the prospect of achieving America's 20-year objective of a Europe whole, free, and at peace. We, therefore, continue to have a profound national interest in supporting the people of Ukraine in their quest for a more stable, democratic, and prosperous future. In this effort, we deeply appreciate Congress' bipartisan attention and support.

The CHAIRMAN. Secretary Glaser.

STATEMENT OF HON. DANIEL L. GLASER, ASSISTANT SECRETARY FOR TERRORIST FINANCING, U.S. DEPARTMENT OF TREASURY, WASHINGTON, DC

Mr. GLASER. Thank you, Chairman Menendez, Ranking Member Corker, and distinguished members of this committee, for inviting me to speak to you again about the administration's response to Russia's occupation and purported annexation of Crimea, and its continued provocative actions elsewhere in eastern Ukraine.

In my remarks today, I will discuss our continuing efforts to impose additional costs on those who seek to destabilize eastern Ukraine and maintain the occupation of Crimea. I will describe the impact that our actions have had on those targeted, as well as on the already faltering Russian economy. I will also discuss the support we and the international community have provided to Ukraine for its economic recovery.

President Obama has issued three Executive orders granting Treasury authority to target those responsible for ongoing unrest in eastern Ukraine. We have now issued five rounds of designations under those Executive orders, responding to the actions of Russia and Russian-backed separatists in Ukraine, designating a total of 52 individuals and 19 entities, including four banks. In so doing, we have sought to have the greatest impact on those whose actions have threatened the sovereignty and territorial integrity of Ukraine, mainly separatist leaders, members of Putin's inner circle and the entities that support them, and Russian Government officials. Our actions have been complemented by designations announced by other countries, including the EU, Canada, and Australia.

Most recently, on June 20, Treasury designated seven individuals who attempted to establish illegal governments in eastern Ukraine or assisted in arming separatist groups. The United States is working with Ukrainian authorities to identify and disrupt financing to those and other separatists.

As President Obama has stated repeatedly, the United States remains prepared to impose additional sanctions, should circumstances warrant. Currently, we are developing a number of options, in the event Russia does not take immediate steps toward de-escalation, including actions involving a broad range of sectors. Of course, such preparation involves close consultation with our partners to maximize the impact on the Russian economy. In the past 2 weeks alone, I have personally traveled to France, Germany, and the U.K. to advance preparations. As Secretary Liu has said, ''If the moment comes when we need to take additional steps, we will be prepared to do so.''

Our measures and the threat of future measures have exacerbated preexisting vulnerabilities of a Russian economy weakened by years of mismanagement. IMF growth projections have been downgraded twice this year and currently are close to zero. The uncertainty created by the combination of Russia's conduct in Ukraine and the ongoing threat of sanctions has led to challenges for Russia's economic outlook, its most prominent companies, and its economic policymakers.

President Putin himself has said that Western sanctions imposed on Russia have had real impact on domestic businesses, including limiting access to funding for many Russian companies. As recently as this week, Russian Deputy Finance Minister Sergei Storchak conceded that Western sanctions are having a significant impact on the Russian economy. He went on to say that, ''The effect of sanctions has intensified because of the imposition of sanctions coincided with the fall in the growth rate of the Russian economy.'' Indeed, we have witnessed more than $50 billion in capital flight this year, and the IMF and the Russian Central Bank project that net outflows will reach $100 billion for the full year.

Increased risk premiums have caused a spike in borrowing costs, shutting many Russian companies out of external debt markets. While Russian politicians project confidence in the face of sanctions, their government's actions show otherwise. The Russian Central Bank has raised key interest rates twice this year, and spent approximately $30 billion on foreign exchange reserves since March to stabilize the ruble amid heavy capital outflows in the first quarter. Despite these interventions, the Russian ruble has depreciated by 5 percent since the beginning of the year. President Putin admitted, last month, that the Government of Russia may need to intervene with budget funds to support Russia's banks.

As a result of sanctions, the Russian Government has openly discussed diverting government funds to support Russian industry. Recently, President Putin stated that Russia needs to look into recapitalizing Gazprom by the amount it would cost to build infrastructure in the Far East.

Taken as a whole, these measures indicate that the Russian Government is focused on short-term crisis-fighting and that its actions are costing Russia the investment needed to reverse long-term downward economic trends.

In addition to our measures to isolate the Russian economy, the United States Government is working with the international community to support Ukrainian Government in returning the country's economy to solid footing. We are working with the IMF, World Bank, and others to ensure that Ukraine has the support it needs over the coming months, as I outline in greater detail in my written testimony.

By combining our efforts to impose financial costs on those threatening peace and security in Ukraine with measures to encourage Ukrainian economic recovery, the United States Government is working to contribute to the development of a strong, unified, and prosperous Ukraine.

Furthermore, we are prepared to take additional strong measures to impose severe costs on Russia in defense of Ukraine's sovereignty and territorial integrity.

Chairman Menendez, I would be happy to answer any questions.

[The prepared statement of Mr. Glaser follows:]

PREPARED STATEMENT OF DANIEL L. GLASER

Chairman Menendez, Ranking Member Corker, and distinguished members of this committee, thank you for inviting me to speak to you again about the administration's response to Russia's occupation and purported annexation of Crimea and its continued provocative actions elsewhere in eastern Ukraine.

In my remarks today, I will describe our continuing efforts to impose additional costs on those who seek to destabilize eastern Ukraine and maintain the occupation of Crimea. I will describe the impact that our actions have had on those targeted, as well as on an already faltering Russian economy. I will also discuss the support that we and the international community have provided to Ukraine for its economic recovery.

IMPOSING COSTS FOR CONTINUED INSTABILITY IN UKRAINE

The President has issued three Executive orders granting Treasury authority to target those responsible for ongoing unrest in eastern Ukraine and Russia's purported annexation of Crimea. We have now issued five rounds of designations responding to Russia's actions and Russia-backed separatists in Ukraine, designating a total of 52 individuals and 19 entities, including 4 banks. In so doing, we have sought to have the greatest impact on those whose actions have threatened the peace, security, stability, sovereignty or territorial integrity of Ukraine—mainly separatist leaders, members of Putin's inner circle and the entities that support them, and Russian Government officials. Our actions have been complemented by designations announced by others, including the EU, Canada, and Australia.

Most recently on June 20, Treasury designated seven individuals who attempted to establish illegitimate governments in eastern Ukraine or assisted in arming separatist groups. These include: Denis Pushilin, self-appointed leader of the so-called "Donetsk People's Republic"; Sergei Menyailo, who proclaimed himself "acting governor" of Sevastopol and assisted in the formation of so-called "defense squads" in Sevastopol; and Valery Bolotov, who proclaimed himself "governor" of the Luhansk region and publically "declared war" on the government in Kiev. Additionally, the United States is working with Ukrainian authorities to identify and disrupt financing to these and other separatists.

As President Obama has stated repeatedly, the United States remains prepared to impose additional sanctions should circumstances warrant. Executive Order 13662 authorizes the targeting of individuals and entities operating in sectors of the Russian economy as determined by the Secretary of the Treasury, in consultation with the Secretary of State. Currently, we are developing a number of options to take action under this authority in the event Russia does not take immediate steps toward de-escalation, including actions involving a broad range of sectors. Of course, such preparation involves close consultation and coordination with our EU, G7, and other international partners to maximize the impact on the Russian economy. In the past 2 weeks alone, I have personally traveled to France, Germany, and the U.K. to advance preparations. As Secretary Lew has said, if the moment comes when we need to take additional steps, we will be prepared to do so.

IMPACT OF MEASURES

Our measures and the threat of future measures have exacerbated preexisting vulnerabilities of a Russian economy weakened by years of mismanagement. IMF growth projections have been downgraded twice this year, and currently are close to zero. Moody's and Fitch have revised the outlook on Russia's sovereign BBB rating from stable to negative, while Standard and Poor's downgraded the sovereign rating by one notch to BBB¥, its lowest investment grade category. This downgrade forced similar ratings cuts on such major Russian corporations as Gazprom, Rosneft, and VTB Bank. The uncertainty created by the combination of Russia's conduct in Ukraine—and the ongoing threat of sanctions—has created challenges for Russia's economic outlook, its most prominent companies and its economic policymakers.

President Putin himself has said that Western sanctions imposed on Russia have had real impact on domestic businesses, including limiting access to funding for many Russian companies. As recently as this week, Russian Deputy Finance Minister Sergei Storchak conceded that Western sanctions are having a significant, though indirect, impact on the Russian economy. He went on to say that "the effect of sanctions has intensified because the imposition of sanctions coincided with a fall in the growth rate of the Russian economy."

Indeed, we have witnessed more than $50 billion in capital flight this year and the IMF and Russian Central Bank project that net outflows will reach $100 billion for the full year. The Russian Central Bank has intervened heavily in order to stabilize the ruble amid persistent outflows. Meanwhile, an increase in risk premium caused a spike in borrowing costs shutting many Russian companies out of external debt markets. Russia's Lukoil has indicated that it will cut spending in order to reduce dependency on international debt markets. Furthermore, the bottom lines of key Russian financial institutions demonstrate the effects of a weakening ruble and deteriorating investment climate. In late May, Russia's two largest banks by assets, Sberbank and VTB, reported 18 and 98 percent drops in quarterly profits, respectively. Finally, it is important to note that despite the more recent recovery in asset prices, Russian asset prices continue to underperform relative to their emerging market peers.

While Russian politicians project confidence in the face of sanctions, their government's actions show otherwise. The Russian Central Bank has raised key interest rates twice this year and spent approximately $30 billion in foreign exchange reserves since March to stabilize the ruble, amid heavy capital outflows in the first quarter. Despite these interventions, the Russian ruble has depreciated by 5 percent since the beginning of the year. Likewise credit institutions' liabilities to the Central Bank of Russia have increased by over $30 billion (25 percent) since February. President Putin admitted last month that the Government of Russia may need to intervene with budget funds to support Russia's banks.

As a result of sanctions, the Russian Government has openly discussed diverting government funds to support Russian industry. Recently, President Putin stated that Russia needs to look into recapitalizing Gazprom by the amount it would cost to build infrastructure in the Far East. Likewise, the Russian Ministry of Trade and Industry has proposed an import substitution program increasing annual domestic volume of production by more than $890 million starting from 2015 in order to offset import losses. Taken as a whole, these measures indicate that the Russian Government is focused on short-term crisis fighting, which in addition to increasing the costs of Russia's decision to intervene in Ukraine, is costing Russia the investment needed to reverse Russia's long-term downward economic trends. To grow, Russia needs foreign direct investment and to integrate with the global economy. As a consequence, the isolation Russia now faces as a result of its actions in Ukraine will have a significant impact on Russia's growth prospects over the medium term.

SUPPORT TO UKRAINE

In addition to our measures to isolate the Russian economy, the United States Government is working with the international community to support the Ukrainian Government in returning the country's economy to a solid footing. The approval on April 30 of a 2-year, $17 billion IMF reform program has unlocked additional bilateral and multilateral financial support and will set Ukraine on a path to sustainable growth. The IMF is at the center of a broader, $27 billion international support package, and is best placed to support Ukraine's implementation of robust and market-oriented reforms. International assistance totaling nearly $6 billion has been disbursed to date. The government successfully issued $1 billion in 5-year, U.S.-backed debt at a reasonable borrowing cost in mid-May. The first review of Ukraine's IMF program began at the end of June, and provided Ukraine fulfills its reform commitments, approximately $2 billion is expected to be provided by the IMF, World Bank, and other donors by the end of July, with additional resources scheduled for disbursement by the end of the year.

Ukraine's new government has already completed key policy reforms that demonstrate its willingness to make the tough decisions necessary to restore economic stability to Ukraine, and this momentum must be maintained. Retail natural gas prices have been increased, a fiscally responsible budget has been passed, the procurement law has been amended to strengthen governance, and the central bank has allowed market forces to determine the value of the currency. Still, significant challenges remain, including continued implementation of difficult reforms by the Ukrainian Government and ensuring Ukraine has a stable supply of gas. At the same time, conflict in eastern Ukraine is taking a significant toll on Ukraine's already vulnerable economy. Economic activity in parts of eastern Ukraine has ground to a halt and the security situation is undermining confidence and international investment. We are working with the IMF, World Bank, and others to ensure Ukraine has the support it needs over the coming months.

To complement this international financial assistance, expert advisors from Treasury's Office of Technical Assistance have been deployed to Kiev to help the Ukrainian authorities stabilize the financial sector and implement reforms. Treasury advisors are working closely with the Finance Ministry, National Bank of Ukraine, and Deposit Guarantee Fund to develop strategies to manage public sector debt, resolve failed banks, improve banking supervision, and spur financial intermediation.

CONCLUSION

By combining our efforts to impose financial costs on those threatening peace and security in Ukraine with measures to encourage Ukrainian economic recovery, the United States Government is working to contribute to the development of a strong, unified, and prosperous Ukraine. Furthermore, we are prepared to take additional strong measures to impose severe costs on Russia in defense of Ukraine's sovereignty and territorial integrity.

The CHAIRMAN. Thank you.
Secretary Chollet.

STATEMENT OF HON. DEREK CHOLLET, ASSISTANT SECRETARY OF DEFENSE FOR INTERNATIONAL SECURITY AFFAIRS, U.S. DEPARTMENT OF DEFENSE, WASHINGTON, DC

Mr. CHOLLET. Thanks. Mr. Chairman, Ranking Member Corker, members of the committee, thank you for inviting me here today to discuss the ongoing crisis in Ukraine and how the Department of Defense is working to help Ukraine address its security needs.

We remain deeply concerned by the security situation in Ukraine's east, where the Russian military remains very active in facilitating the movement of forces, equipment, and finances across the border. Additionally, Russian irregular forces and Russian-backed local separatists remain active inside eastern Ukraine, and both are supported by Russian financing. These actions are not consistent with Russia's pledge to stabilize the situation and seek a negotiated outcome.

It is in our interest to have a Ukraine that is stable and secure. Across the spectrum, Ukrainian leaders have made clear that they want our help, and we are committed to assisting them, which is a message that President Obama, Vice President Biden, Secretaries Kerry and Hagel have made clear in their meetings with their Ukrainian counterparts in the past month.

On security, we are working to support Ukraine along three lines of effort.

First, we will continue to support Ukraine's urgent supply needs. President Obama has approved $33 million in security assistance for Ukraine since the beginning of the crisis. This is an order of magnitude beyond our assistance in previous years to Ukraine, and more than four times what we provided Ukraine last year. This assistance has started to flow. We have delivered 2,000 sets of body armor, first aid kits, tactical radios, and 5,000 uniforms. Soon, we will send night-vision devices, thermal imagers, EOD robots, Kevlar helmets, and additional radios. We are actively pursuing additional sources of assistance, which we will apply to Ukraine's most pressing needs.

Second, beyond the immediate supply needs, the Ukrainian military needs support through enhanced training and exercises. As President Obama made clear after his meeting with President Poroshenko last month, we are discussing additional steps to help train and professionalize Ukraine's military. To aid this effort, U.S. European Command has established a Senior Steering Committee with Ukrainian counterparts to identify areas where we can improve our bilateral military cooperation, conduct assessments, and identify requirements we can address through training and development. And those meetings are underway in Kiev this week.

Third, and perhaps most importantly, we will work with Ukraine on reforming and, in some cases, rebuilding its defense institutions. While I was in Kiev last month, meeting with Ukrainian Defense and National Security officials, the Ukrainian Defense Minister said that the biggest obstacle to reform is the military mind-set still largely oriented toward the old Soviet way of doing things. And he requested our assistance in reform and improving military education. To do so, United States defense advisors will help the Ukrainians develop a feasible and sustainable reform program. To get this started, a five-member initial scoping team visited Kiev a few weeks ago and met with various Ukrainian defense and security officials.

Additionally, embedded United States civilian advisors in the Ukrainian Defense Ministry can help the government build a national security strategy that provides a cohesive vision for the Ukrainian military, border guards, national guard, and other security institutions.

Another area of needed reform will be in the defense industry. Ukraine is endowed with an advanced defense industrial base, that employs more than 40,000 people, which is in danger of collapse due to the current reliance on the Russian market. Given Russia's aggressive actions in Crimea, Donetsk, and Lugansk, and elsewhere, the Ukrainian Government has understandably stopped all military sales to Russia. To reverse the downward trend in the Ukrainian defense industry, United States advisors can help

Ukrainians develop long-term investment plans to enable them to attract other markets, develop long-term investment plans, and shift away from reliance on Russia.

Mr. Chairman, members of this committee, the United States cannot achieve success in these three areas of security assistance by itself. We need others to join us. For example, NATO allies who have experienced their own challenging defense reforms over the past decade, such as Poland and the Baltic States, can provide abundant expertise on similar reforms in Ukraine. And we need other NATO allies to step up and help Ukraine security forces to continue to reform and modernize and professionalize over the medium to long term.

We will also continue to rely on the leadership from Congress, especially in supporting the European Reassurance Initiative, which President Obama announced on his trip to Europe last month. If approved, this initiative of $1 billion will help the U.S. military to increase its defense presence in Europe and would cover enhanced training, readiness, exercises, and facility improvements in Europe to reassure our allies. The initiative would also bolster our materiel assistance to key partners, such as Ukraine.

So, I look forward to working with this committee, and the Congress as a whole, as we seek your approval on this important effort. Thank you, and I look forward to your questions.

[The prepared statement of Mr. Chollet follows:]

PREPARED STATEMENT OF DEREK CHOLLET

Chairman Menendez, Ranking Member Corker, and committee members, thank you for inviting me to discuss the ongoing crisis in Ukraine, which was precipitated by Russia's occupation of Crimea and its ongoing destabilization campaign in eastern Ukraine. Today I will update you on the multiple lines of effort that the Department of Defense is pursuing to help Ukraine meet its immediate security needs, and also to help Ukraine develop a more professional and capable military for the future.

We are many months into the crisis, and Russia's actions are as unacceptable today as they were in February. Our commander in Europe, General Breedlove, succinctly described Russia's posture and actions in a recent press conference. He said that Russian regular forces are very active along the border of Ukraine facilitating the movement of forces, equipment, and finances across the border. Russian irregular forces, and Russian-led and -backed local separatists, are active inside eastern Ukraine, and they are supported by Russian financing. These actions fly in the face of international commitments and standards governing relations among states, so we have taken concerted actions as a government to raise Russia's costs for these blatantly unacceptable actions.

I visited Kiev just before the inauguration of Ukraine's new President Poroshenko in June. Across the spectrum, Ukrainian leaders made clear that they continue to want the U.S. Government's help, and I assured them that we are committed to assisting them. Ukraine matters. It is a European nation, bordering NATO member states. The Ukrainian people freely elected a new President who has pledged to fulfill their desire to increase cooperation with Europe both politically and economically, and who has just signed a trade agreement with the European Union to accelerate that process. Ukraine has a long history of security cooperation with the United States, and it has been a steadfast coalition partner in Afghanistan, Iraq, Kosovo, and Bosnia, as well as in counterpiracy operations off the Horn of Africa.

We want Ukraine to continue on this trajectory, and to do so we're helping in three ways.

First, though we have been clear that there is no military solution to this crisis, Ukraine has the right to restore order and stability within its territory through the use of its armed forces, internal security forces, and border guards. Before he met with Ukrainian President Poroshenko in June, President Obama approved an additional tranche of $5 million in nonlethal security assistance for Ukraine on June 4, and Vice President Biden announced an additional $10 million for assistance to the

State Border Guard Service on June 7, bringing the total since the beginning of the crisis to $33 million currently being used for nonlethal security assistance.

During the months of June and July, nonlethal assistance started to flow. For example:

- 1,929 first aid kits were delivered to the military hospital in Kharkiv, in eastern Ukraine, in late June.
- 80 multiband handheld radios, including batteries, arrived in Kiev in late June, as did 1,000 sleeping mats and over 5,000 uniform items.
- We completed delivery of 2,000 body armor vests to Ukraine on July 4.

Over the next 2 months, we will purchase and ship 150 night-vision devices, 150 thermal imagers, 1,000 Kevlar helmets, 5 explosive ordnance disposal robots, and another 96 radios.

Second, beyond immediate needs, the Ukrainian military requires support through training and exercises. Ukraine has been a member of NATO's Partnership for Peace since 1994, and it has a long history of hosting bilateral exercises with the United States and multilateral exercises with NATO member states. But prior Ukrainian Governments, especially that led by former President Yanukovych, starved the military not only of modern equipment, but also of sufficient training. The new Ukrainian Government, under President Poroshenko, is clear about its desire for more military cooperation, including training and development. The U.S. European Command (USEUCOM) has established a senior steering committee with Ukrainian counterparts to identify areas where we can improve our bilateral military cooperation, conduct assessments, and identify requirements we can address through training and development.

Third, and perhaps most importantly, we will work with Ukraine on reforming and, in some cases, rebuilding its defense institutions. We must help Ukraine spend its defense budget more wisely, plan for a new navy to replace the naval assets unlawfully seized by Russia, and expand and empower a cadre of noncommissioned officers. While I was in Kiev, senior Ministry of Defense officials said that the biggest obstacle to reform is a military mindset that is still largely oriented toward the old, Soviet way of doing things, and requested our assistance in improving military education. To do so, advisors from the Department of Defense, including USEUCOM, will help the Ukrainians develop a feasible and sustainable reform program. A five-member initial scoping team, composed of civilian Defense personnel and contracting experts, visited Kiev on June 15–19 and met with various Ukrainian defense and security officials. Also, embedded U.S. civilian advisors in the Ukrainian Defense Ministry will help the government build a national security strategy that provides a cohesive vision for the Ukrainian Armed Forces, border guards, National Guard, and other security institutions.

Another area of beneficial reform will be in the defense industry. Ukraine is endowed with a strong and advanced defense industrial base—employing more than 40,000 people—which is in danger of collapse due to its current reliance on the Russian market. Due to Russia's aggressive actions in Crimea, Donetsk, and Luhansk, the Ukrainian Government has understandably stopped all military sales to Russia. U.S. advisors can help them diversify this industry to attract other markets, develop long-term investment plans, and shift away from reliance on Russia.

The United States cannot realize success in these three areas of security assistance by itself. We need others to join us. New NATO allies who have experienced their own challenging defense reforms over the past decade, such as Poland and the Baltic States, can provide abundant expertise on similar reforms for Ukraine. We will engage with these allies and others to build a comprehensive and multifaceted approach to help Ukraine defend itself adequately, and become a more secure and capable partner.

Chairman Menendez, Ranking Member Corker, and committee members, we need Congress' help too. The administration recently announced its European Reassurance Initiative (ERI), which was reflected in the budget amendment submitted last month. If approved, this $1 billion initiative would help the Department increase its defense presence in Europe and would cover enhanced training, readiness, exercises, and facility improvements in Europe to reassure our allies. In addition, ERI funds could be used to bolster our material assistance to key partners such as Ukraine, so I urge congressional approval of this important proposal.

Thank you for your time. I look forward to your questions.

The CHAIRMAN. Well, thank you all.

Let me start with you, Secretary Nuland. A month ago, President Obama and the G7 promised more economic sanctions if Putin did not stop inciting violence in eastern Ukraine. In a pattern that seems increasingly familiar to all of us, Putin made gestures that suggested the appearance of Russian withdrawal, while simultaneously engaging in other actions, such as having tanks cross the border and overseeing the cutoff to gas supplies, that are hostile by anyone's standard. And then, reading from your testimony, Russia has made too many commitments at the diplomatic table over the past 4 months that have been rendered hollow by the weapons, cash, and fighters that continue to flow across the border to fuel the fight in eastern Ukraine. And that element was also echoed by Secretary Chollet.

So, I look at what the standards were, which was calling on Russia to end all support for separatists to control the border, to help establish an effective OSCE monitoring regime, to use its influence with separatists to return the three border checkpoints to Ukrainian authorities, to release the hostages they hold, to launch substantial negotiations on the implementation of President Poroshenko's peace plan. And yet I see no advance in any of those standards.

So, what are we waiting for?

Ms. NULAND. Thank you, Chairman.

Well, I certainly do not disagree with your assessment that we have not seen progress on any of the areas that I outlined or, indeed, that the G7 outlined or that the EU Council outlined. As I said, when President Poroshenko came into office, he came in with his broad and deep peace plan and was committed to testing it. His first aspiration was to test it in concert with separatists. So, he first wanted to try to negotiate a cease-fire that was bilateral. When, after a couple of weeks of effort, that failed, he decided to initiate his cease-fire unilaterally. And that was a test that he asked the United States and Europe to support, to see whether separatists would meet him halfway, to see whether, in fact, Russia would meet him halfway after the meeting at Normandy, brokered by Chancellor Merkel, President Hollande, between President Putin and President Poroshenko. As you have noted—and as I noted in my testimony—that cease-fire came and went, and, in the process, Ukraine lost territory to separatists, it lost border control posts, and the weapons continued to flow.

The Europeans continue to try to bring the sides together to see if a cease-fire can be reestablished. They have failed, over the last week, to do that, because separatists have refused to meet in any location that is safe.

So, we are continuing to consult with our European allies. The President, the Secretary, all of us, have been in constant day-by-day discussion with the Europeans to assess. And I think our analysis is the same, that we have not seen progress.

So, in that context, we are continuing to prepare the next round of sanctions. As we have said repeatedly, and as the President has said, these sanctions will be more effective, they will be stronger, if the United States and Europe work together. And we——

The CHAIRMAN. But, it begs——

Ms. NULAND [continuing]. Are working on those.

The CHAIRMAN. I appreciate your answer, and I have let you go, to try to make it as substantive as possible, but it begs the question, what are we waiting for? I understand all of that. I think the

Ukrainian Government has bent over backward to try to get to a peaceful resolution that will get the Russians to ultimately go along. But, all the Russians call for are cease-fires, and then they take advantage of it, and they do nothing in return.

What is this about a Ukrainian fighter pilot turning up in Russian jails? How does Russia justify having a Ukrainian Armed Force member acquired by separatists ending up in a Russian jail? How is that an example of trying to resolve the problem?

Ms. NULAND. Well, thank you for citing that case, which is clearly a violation of international law and human rights. This is a Ukrainian servicemember who was taken hostage on the battlefield by separatists about a month ago, and she has now turned up, as you said, in a Russian prison, clearly making obvious that link between Russia and separatists.

Senator, we are continuing the conversation with the Europeans about the right moment for sanctions as they prepare for the last meeting of European heads before the summer break, which is on July 16.

The CHAIRMAN. So, if, per chance, on July 16, the European Union heads do not come to a conclusion and move forward on sanctions, which is only about less than a week away or so, then will we have the summer lapse, and Putin will know that there are no consequences, and the United States will stay on the sidelines, waiting for the Europeans? Is that something that we could actually expect?

Ms. NULAND. Chairman, as I said, our goal is to act in concert with Europe, but the President has always made clear that, if necessary, he will act on our own.

The CHAIRMAN. Let me ask you this. We see the Russians creating a cessation of oil deliveries and gas deliveries to the Ukraine. And I would love to hear what that looks like, going into the fall, if it continues, which will not be too far in the distance. We have American companies helping Russia learn how to drill offshore in the Arctic and exploit their shale resources. Now, I do not think we should necessarily create a Russian shale revolution and thereby strengthen Russia's energy weapon, which they have shown clearly that they are willing to use, and threaten others in Europe to do. Where is the administration on that issue?

Ms. NULAND. Chairman, we have made clear to U.S. business the risks of continuing to provide high-tech investment in the current climate. We have also, in the context of our sanctions work internally and with the Europeans, focused intensively on what we might do in the next round with regard to high-technology investment. You are not wrong that Russia depends on outside investment in order to take its energy exports to the next level and to——

The CHAIRMAN. You know, Russia is basically an extracting country. It does not create too much more. And that is the biggest driver of its economy. It seems to me that if the Russians have shown themselves willing to use energy as a weapon, which they have—Ukraine is the perfect example of it, but even the European reticence is, in large part, about energy questions—then, at the end of the day, why would the United States, with all of its national interests and national security interests, allow entities to ultimately help the Russians further develop their energy resources so that they would have more energy to be able to use as a weapon? Is anybody thinking about that?

Ms. NULAND. We are thinking about that, Chairman. This is in the category of a set of measures one could take that would only be effective, in terms of the goal that you seek, if they were done in concert with Europe, because, while the United States has this technology, so do some key European companies, as well, and we would not want to be in a situation of denying our companies and having Europeans backfill.

The CHAIRMAN. But, I think there is——

Ms. NULAND. So, we are having a conversation——

The CHAIRMAN [continuing]. Right now——

Ms. NULAND [continuing]. With Europe about it.

The CHAIRMAN. And I doubt that there is anyone in the world as advanced as the United States on the specific technologies as it relates to shale exploration. It seems to me that we fight with one hand behind our back, maybe two, with a leader who has no limitations, from what I can gather, other than when he is faced with an equivalent countervailing force that is either military—and which we are not talking about, in this case—or economic. And so I do not get it. I do not know how much longer there are going to be those of us willing to wait before we act independently.

Senator Corker.

Senator CORKER. Thank you, Mr. Chairman. And some of your questions really are the kind of questions I want to pursue.

And, Secretary Nuland, I know that you do a good job of staying in touch with us, and I appreciate that. And yet, seriously, I sometimes wonder whether Foreign Service officers feel like resigning when you are put out there to continue to sort of sound tough, but know that nothing is really going to happen.

I am just curious, knowing that you are serving in the State Department and have responsibilities, if you, to the degree that you can, would tell us what really is happening here with the sanctions? The fact is, everything we said we were going to put sanctions in place for, relative to Russian actions, has occurred. Every single thing. They have never responded to the threats, the hollow threats that we put out there. What is really driving our sort of feckless sanctions policy right now? Is it the internal debate in the administration between the economic folks, who are so worried about the elections this fall that they do not want to do anything that might blow back on us economically, and the security folks, who are concerned about that very bitter peace that we are basically establishing right now with Russia? Is that what is driving it? Or is it the fact that we know Europe is never going to come to the table?

What is keeping us from doing some of the things that the chairman has mentioned, that I have talked to you about on the phone? What is keeping us from going ahead and putting sanctions in place, when we know that there is Russian military equipment on the ground in eastern Ukraine? You all know that, and have said it publicly. They are funding separatists. What else is it that we need to see happen and know happen before we actually put biting sanctions in place?

Ms. NULAND. Well, first of all, Chairman, just to say, it is my great honor to serve in this position at this very vital moment.

Senator CORKER. I know it has to be very frustrating, though, to continue to wake up in the mornings and look in the mirror and practice talking tough, but know that nothing is going to happen. I really respect your service. I would just love for you to share with me why nothing is happening.

Ms. NULAND. First, Ranking Member Corker, I think it is important to go back and look at the last few months and take some appropriate look at what might have happened, had we not had the rounds of sanctions that we have had.

Senator CORKER. I do not want to hear that. I read the papers, and I talk to you. Tell me what the rub is within the administration that is keeping it continuing to lay out redlines and make threats, but not act, continuing to undermine our credibility, continuing to move toward this bitter peace I alluded to. Tell me what is keeping us from taking action today like putting military equipment on the ground. We know they are funding separatists. We know they are playing this duplicitous game of escalation and de-escalation. Why are we not acting?

Ms. NULAND. Again, as I said, with regard to this next round, it was the desire, first, of President Poroshenko, to test his peace plan. He has now done that. We are quite clear that we have not seen the results that we are seeking from Russia, so we are now talking to the Europeans about when it is appropriate to move together. As I said——

Senator CORKER. When is it appropriate?

Ms. NULAND. As I said, their last heads meeting of the summer is next week. It is on July 16. And they very much—and we very much—prefer to move together.

Senator CORKER. Yes.

Ms. NULAND. So, we are looking at the evidence, and we are building the package as we move forward.

Senator CORKER. You remember you told me, that the last meeting we were going to have was the end of June. And that is when we were going to take action. And I know that everybody on this panel has to be incredibly frustrated. Again, so we can understand the dynamic within the White House, within the administration, I just wish that you would explain to me what it is, internally, that is keeping us from going ahead and putting sanctions in place, when we know exactly what is happening.

Ms. NULAND. I think the primary desire, at the moment, is to stay tightly coordinated with Europe as we move forward, because the sanctions will be stronger if we move together.

But, Chairman, if I might, for a minute, just remind that we—you know, there was a moment, where we had 40,000 Russian troops ringing the border. We threatened sanctions, and those troops moved back——

Senator CORKER. That is absolutely untrue. That is absolutely untrue. They stayed on the border——

Ms. NULAND. Some of them——

Senator CORKER [continuing]. Weeks and weeks and weeks afterward. And they kept saying they were moving away, and our

NATO friends kept saying they are not moving away. That is absolutely not true, what you just said.

Ms. NULAND. There was a moment when we had 40,000 combat units ready to move. A lot of them moved back, but you are not wrong that we have a significant number returned. There was a time when we thought we would not have an election in Ukraine. And it was the solidarity between the United States and Europe, including the threat of sanctions, that helped preserve the space for those elections.

So, we have, when we work together with Europe, been able to provide time and space for Ukraine to recover. We need to, to the extent that we can, continue to work with Europe, because that will make this policy as effective as possible.

Senator CORKER. I am embarrassed for us. And I just wish the administration would quit saying publicly, through you and others, the things that are being said, when we know that we are not going to act. We do not act.

Secretary Glaser, you talk about the damage we have done to the economy. I just had someone look—and maybe we read the chart wrong—and I just looked at it briefly, and I apologize for not having done it an hour or so ago—but, the Russian stock market is up 22 percent since March. Whenever I talk to people at the White House, they tell me how damaging this has been to the Russian economy, and then I keep citing stats that point to something very, very different.

Am I correct that the Russian stock market is up 22 percent since March? Am I reading the chart wrong?

Mr. GLASER. The Russian stock market is up. I do not know if that is the exact right number, but I am sure that is correct.

Senator CORKER. Okay.

Mr. GLASER. But——

Senator CORKER. So, just out of curiosity—I know there are a few oligarchs, that probably are having some unpleasant travel experiences and maybe having some assets frozen. But, how is this affecting Putin's calculation, when the economy is booming? Because I guess people around the world realize that our threats are hollow, that we are never going to do anything. Germany sees itself as a bridge between us and Russia. Chairman and I were at a dinner one night, where that was clearly pointed out. They are not going to take action. So, how can you say that the sanctions that we have put in place already have had any effect whatsoever on Russian behavior?

Mr. GLASER. Well, thank you for the question, Mr. Senator.

I do not think that short-term gains in the Russian stock market counterbalance the long-term real damage that we have done, and are continuing to do, to the Russian economy. That is been recognized by the Russian Government, as I note in my testimony. It is recognized by foreign investors, as demonstrated by the fact that Russian businesses, Russians banks, are having a hard time raising capital in international capital markets. It is recognized by the Russian people, themselves, as reflected by the $50 billion in capital flight we have seen already, estimated to be at $100 billion by the end of the year. So, that is the Russian Government, the Russian people, and international investors, who all recognize that the Russian economy has been severely damaged, both by Russian mismanagement and by our sanctions and threat of future sanctions.

So, I do think that we could point to real impact that we have had. And I think it is a fair question, At what point does this start to impact Russian strategic calculations? And you are absolutely correct. I do think that, at this point, as Toria said, we have had some deterrent impact on Russia, particularly in terms of tactics. But, it is clear to all of us that, as a broad strategic matter, their strategy remains the same. And that is why, as Toria said, we are working so hard internally and working so hard with our friends and partners in Europe and in the G7 to make sure that, when the time comes, we have a very strong package of measures. And I am quite confident that, at that time, we will have a strong package of measures, and it will do severe damage to the Russian economy.

Senator CORKER. Mr. Chairman, thank you for the time.

I just want to close by saying that, again, I respect each of your service to our country. I know that each of you have to be somewhat disappointed in the actions that have not been taken.

And, Secretary Chollet, I mean, $33 million in assistance to the Ukrainian military, I think that is nice. We still have not done the things that they have really asked us to do.

And I would just say, to Secretary Glaser, the damage you are talking about that the Russian economy will see, I think our country acting like such a paper tiger to the world on this and so many other fronts is doing incredible long-term damage to our Nation. And I do hope, at some point, the administration will actually follow through on the things that it continues to tout publicly.

Thank you, Mr. Chairman.

The CHAIRMAN. Senator Shaheen.

Senator SHAHEEN. Thank you, Mr. Chairman.

Thank you all for being here.

Secretary Chollet, there were a number of reports over the weekend about successes of the Ukrainian military. And I wonder if you could talk a little bit about how substantive we think those successes were, what we attribute those to, and what response we are seeing out of Russia.

Mr. CHOLLET. Thanks, Senator.

You are absolutely right, there have been, over the last 4 or 5 days, some significant successes by the Ukrainian military in the east. A major city, Slovyansk, was liberated and is in control now of the Ukrainians. There are several other key cities that are now largely surrounded by the Ukrainian military. We are watching that situation very closely.

I think there is probably not one single answer to why we have seen the tide turn, at least for the moment. And I want to stress that we are not—this is not over yet. So, although the trendline is good for now, we need to watch this very closely. It could be that the cease-fire period allowed the Ukrainian military to regroup, orient itself. As you have seen, President Poroshenko has been very active in the planning and the leadership of this. He was, just yesterday, dressed in military fatigues in the field, talking to his troops and his generals.

But also, I think you can see that, although there is a significant Russian presence on the border, that has been reduced. We are still seeing weapons appear on one side of the border, and then mysteriously appear on the other side of the border, that are clearly Russian origin.

But, so, I think it is a combination of a little bit of a lessening of support by Russia, but then also an opportunity for the Ukrainians to regroup after this very quickly cascading crisis over the previous months. The cease-fire, I think helped.

Senator SHAHEEN. Well, again, if I could ask you to answer on what do we think—why do we think Russia has pulled back somewhat, and what do we think their continued response will be if the Ukrainian military continues to be successful?

Mr. CHOLLET. So, on why Russia has pulled back, I do think the sanctions have helped. I think this was—they did have an effect, and they certainly changed Putin's calculation on how much support he would be willing to give and how deep he would get into this. The Ukrainians have also been able to improve their border security. They have said that their border is sealed along the east. That has been a very porous border. When I was there, a month ago, and was briefed by the head of the Border Security, it was described how, in many cases, it is not even demarcated, the border between Ukraine and Russia, so that I think that has helped.

I think we have to be very mindful of what the Russian response could be, and that is why we are watching this so closely. It is a very dangerous situation. And, of course, the Ukrainians need to be vigilant, themselves, on how they handle the situation, in terms of civilian casualties in the surrounding of these cities. And they have stressed to us that they are going to be very careful about how they handle this situation.

But, I think we have to really expect the worst, in terms of Russian response; and that is why we are watching it so closely.

Senator SHAHEEN. Secretary Nuland, can I ask you to respond to that, too? Assuming that the Ukrainians continue to be successful in throwing the rebels out of the cities that they are holding and actually forcing them, many of whom are Russian, back into Russia, what do we think Putin's response will be? And are we concerned that their success means that Russia will be more aggressive in coming into eastern Ukraine?

Ms. NULAND. Again, Senator, I think it depends on how Putin ultimately calculates his interests. He has other ways to create pressure and destabilization on Ukraine, including the energy card and the economic card. But, our hope would be that, as the Ukrainians, as Assistant Secretary Chollet said, harden the border and make it more difficult to covertly support the separatists, that the choices become more stark for Russia, at least on the military side.

Another factor that I think has contributed to the Ukrainian success is that, in the towns that separatists have held, Slovyansk and Kramatorsk before they were liberated, human rights abuses, looting, abuse of the civilian population have gravely turned those in the east who may have had affinity toward Russia, who may have had affinity toward the separatists' agenda at the beginning, firmly against them. And the Ukrainian military has benefited from improved intelligence from the population that wants these guys gone.

So, it is a matter of the Ukrainians continuing to deploy careful, judicious tactics to make a success and restore good livelihood in places like Kramatorsk and Slovyansk, that are free, and make them an example in Donetsk, but also continuing to raise the cost of military intervention by raising that border, by making it clear that, in the international community, we will sanction against more military—more transfers of heavy metal and those kinds of things.

Senator SHAHEEN. And are we seeing Poroshenko being willing to address corruption within the country? And what kinds of concrete steps has he taken and has he committed to take?

Ms. NULAND. The government, just last week, published its 3-year anticorruption plan and its 6-month action plan. As you know, Senator, they have already started to put a legislative base in place through the Rada that was part of the IMF conditionality. There is more legislative base required as part of their association with the European Union. The key focuses of the 6-month action plan are preventing conflict of interest for public servants, strengthening punishment for corruption, judicial reform, going after some of the most corrupt folks in the system, e-governance, creating transparency, those kinds of things. And we are committing significant U.S. assistance to help in the anticorruption effort, as is the European Union. But, we will have to judge them by how they implement. It is a very difficult, pernicious problem throughout society, as you know.

Senator SHAHEEN. And is that an agenda that is helpful as they are taking back cities in eastern Ukraine, to be able to show very specific actions? And are they willing to do that? And do they have support from local officials in those communities?

Ms. NULAND. It was the number one plank on which President Poroshenko ran for office. Anticorruption, clean government, clean Ukraine, Europe, and peace—those were his three platforms. So, they have now got to prove it on all sides.

In eastern Ukraine, the number one concern is economic opportunity and the fact that it is been, essentially, a rust-belt, heavy-industry economy. So, as the Ukrainian Government takes back parts of eastern Ukraine, they are reaching out to us, they are reaching out to the European Union, asking for support for micro-projects and other things that will quickly jump-start the economy and, over the longer term, diversification of that economy away from heavy industry and extractive, and into things that will bring innovation and technology and opportunity to the Donbas.

Senator SHAHEEN. My time is up. Thank you.

I would suggest that energy efficiency, as they are looking at projects, is one great opportunity that they should take advantage of.

The CHAIRMAN. Senator Flake.

Senator FLAKE. Thank you.

Secretary Nuland, I think we are all buoyed by what we have heard in the last couple of weeks, particularly the military successes, and how we attribute that. I think we are all surprised that the Ukrainian military is showing more strength then they seemed to have before. But also, I think a lot of it is the fact that the elections were good, went well, the government has legitimacy, people have some hope, in the east at least. With regard to further action by the Russians and their calculations and our own sanctions, I could not agree more that the sanctions are more effective, I have always felt, in other areas of the world as well, when they are multilateral, not unilateral. And it is far more effective if we work hand in glove with Europe.

Say the same situation that we have today, roughly, persists, that Russia kind of plays this game, maybe the Ukrainian military is successful on and off, taking another city or pushing back a little. I just want your honest assessment of where Europe is, here. Will they move forward, imposing tougher sanctions, if we have anything approximating the status quo in Ukraine?

Ms. NULAND. It is my judgment, based on hours and hours and hours of consultation with Europeans and trips across some 20 of the 28 European Union countries, that, if Russia does not stop re-arming separatists, does not stop its financial support, that we will have European support for another round of sanctions. It may not be completely parallel to everything that we want to do, but this is a process moving forward. There is no one in Europe who thinks that what is happening in eastern Ukraine is in the EU's interest or Europe's interest, and everybody wants to get back to a place where there are civilized relations between Russia and Ukraine. So, we have to make it cost if Putin continues to go down that road.

Senator FLAKE. Can you describe, outside of sanctions, what efforts are being made to push back on Russia's failure to—pull back, I should say, further than they have? Aside from sanctions, what efforts is the State Department undertaking?

Ms. NULAND. We have also, working with Europe, put in place an intensive campaign of diplomatic and political and, to some extent, economic isolation. For example, as you know, the United States has ceased virtually all military-to-military cooperation with Russia. We have ceased virtually all economic cooperation at the government level—high technology, all that kind of thing. The Europeans have largely matched that. You will recall that we downgraded the G8 back to a G7, and had it in Brussels without the Russians. None of us, with the exception of Normandy and a couple of other things, have been welcoming senior-level Russians in our capitals. We have been restricting the work we do together to those things that are clearly in our global shared interest.

Senator FLAKE. Mr. Chollet, the Ukrainian military benefits from—I guess it is the Partners for Peace Program with NATO. Can you describe that? How is that helping them prepare and grow and have the capabilities that they need?

Mr. CHOLLET. Absolutely. It has helped them over 20 years that they have been a NATO partner, and they have operated with United States and NATO forces in places like Kosovo and Iraq and Afghanistan still today. And so, there is no doubt that their partnership with NATO has helped them in the course of this crisis. The fact that they were a partner with NATO has helped us diplomatically and militarily, in terms of supporting Ukraine in various meetings in Brussels of both Secretary Kerry and Secretary

Hagel, around the NATO Ukraine Council. So, there is a lot of support that they get, and there is practical help that they get. And NATO—in addition to United States bilateral efforts, NATO is also seeking ways to continue to help Ukraine reform and further professionalize its military.

Senator FLAKE. Is the Ukrainian military and the government satisfied with our efforts to bolster the military there?

Mr. CHOLLET. In my talks, a month ago, with the then-Ukrainian Defense Minister—we have a new Defense Minister—but, as well as the National Security Advisor, we talked a lot about the support that they were looking for, and some of which is support that has been delivered since my visit, particularly in the body armor, which they were very focused on. There are other items that are on the way. We have pledged to do—we can pay for—things like night vision, and border security is something that they are very, very focused on. They have a very long list of asks, as you have probably seen. And part of the point of the discussions that I have had, that Secretary Hagel has had, that our European Command team is having today in Kiev, is to talk with them in more detail about further needs that they have.

Senator FLAKE. All right.

Thank you, Mr. Chairman.

The CHAIRMAN. Senator Murphy.

Senator MURPHY. Thank you very much, Mr. Chairman.

You know, this is not the cold war. The world does not revolve around who is with the United States and who is with Russia any longer. There are paradigms that matter a lot more to us than that. But, it has similarities, in the sense that this is a long-term engagement in which we are creating a contrast with Russia for the countries that lie along the faultline between East and West. And what matters most, really, is the work that we do over years and decades to rebuild the economic and military capacity of those countries so that they truly have a choice.

I join with Senator Corker in lacking envy for the position that you are in, but for different reasons. I think we want to be careful not to be too responsive in the short run so as to pollute the efforts that we need to make in coordination with the Europeans to win the long-term game. The Russians used to be the best at playing the long game; that is how they expelled Napoleon from Russian territory. Today, they are all about short-term return. We now have the advantage, hopefully, of seeing the long-term game.

However, Secretary Nuland, I want to challenge a little bit of your optimism about where Europe is heading. I agree with Senator Flake that we have to do this, to the extent possible, in coordination with Europe. But, they seem to be moving backward in some ways. The French are arming the Russians. There are about a half-dozen EU countries now that are considering building the South Stream Pipeline even though it contravenes the third energy package directives out of the EU. I think that further complicates your work. It is more the reason why I am not envious of the position you are in, because I think that you are working with a continent in which they fundamentally disagree as to what kind of existential threat Russian aggression presents them. We tell them that they have to be serious about this, and they turn around and have a very different view.

So, am I wrong to think that, in some ways, Europe is moving in the wrong direction rather than, in your estimation, kind of holding a neutral position, pending new developments?

Ms. NULAND. Senator, as you know, because you have traveled to a very large number of the countries under my responsibility, there are lots of different views and lots of different situations within Europe, in terms of their historic structural dependency on Russia. What we are trying to do in the conversation is make the point that you have made, that everything is connected to everything, that what we offer is a democratic free-market model, and that is what we need to support in Ukraine, in Moldova, in Georgia.

On things like South Stream, you made a good impact when you were in Bulgaria, and that was very important for U.S. diplomacy. I would, though, give a shout-out also to the EU, which has suspended support for South Stream until it can further evaluate the larger dependency impact of that project. And we are working intensively with the European Union on the larger issue—and with the nation-states—of energy diversification, giving them other options—interconnectors, LNG, other sources of energy to reduce their dependence—major line of effort of what we are involved with.

So, I think it is an issue of continuing to talk to the Europeans about our larger strategic interest of creating less dependency on countries that are autocratic and countries that use trade as a weapon and countries that use energy as a weapon, and more of a vibrant market set of principles within Europe.

Senator MURPHY. My default is to do this in concert with the Europeans, but when we were in Bulgaria, we did see the effect of unilateral United States sanctions. We sanctioned a Russian individual, Timchenko, who was potentially going to be connected to the construction of the South Stream Pipeline into Bulgaria. I am not exactly sure why Bulgaria decided to halt construction, but there is a lot of speculation that part of it was that they were worried about the consequences of doing business with an individual who was sanctioned unilaterally by the United States.

So, maybe a question to you, Mr. Glaser. As you think about the impact of unilateral sanctions, there certainly seems to be some evidence that, if the Europeans are not willing to move with us, that there is some impact when the United States acts alone.

Mr. GLASER. Absolutely, Mr. Senator. And, as Assistant Secretary Nuland said, President Obama has repeatedly emphasized that we will be prepared to act alone if we need to act alone. And, you are right, the United States plays a pivotal role in the international economy, we play a pivotal role in the international financial system, and that does give us power, and it gives us leverage. And it is leverage that we have been using, as you point out, Mr. Senator, in the case of Russia, frankly, through many of our sanctions programs across a wide range of issues. We have repeatedly shown that, when we act alone, we can act in a meaningful way and we can have real consequences, as I tried to outline in my testimony.

All that said, as you point out, it is obviously the case that we will be more effective and more powerful, both politically and as a practical matter, if we move forward with the European Union, if we move forward with the G7. So, I do think that the time spent trying to put all that together is time well spent.

Senator MURPHY. And listen, by the way, we have a lot of other irons in the fire when it comes to the work that the State Department is doing with Europe, some that actually matter more to United States national security interests than Ukraine. For instance, the Iranian nuclear negotiations.

We had a great hearing yesterday, Secretary Nuland, on European energy security. And thank you for sending your Deputy to join us. Last question, for you: There was some dispute amongst our second panel as to who benefits and who is hurt by a continued dispute over gas supply from Russia into Ukraine through to Europe. Some think that that will ultimately hurt Ukraine, because they will be seen as having to make a choice between their own citizens and passing along the gas to Europe. Others thought that maybe that would move Europe more quickly to energy independence if they continue to see the downside of reliance on transit through Ukraine. What is your guess on who stands to lose the most from a prolonged dispute over gas transit through Ukraine?

Ms. NULAND. I would say, in the short run, both Russia and Ukraine lose, because they do not have other options than to deal with each other. And Ukraine, as you know, makes valuable revenue by being a transit country. Over time, Ukraine, obviously, has to focus more effort, and that is part of the assistance that we are providing on diversifying, including diversifying as a transit hub. Does not just have to be a transit hub for Russia; it can also, through reverse flow, be a transit hub into other countries from Europe, if we can energize the market.

But, obviously, the best outcome will be if—with the European Union's help and European Commissioner Ettinger, as you know, is trying to midwife negotiations between Russia and Ukraine—if they can come to an agreement on a fair European market price in stable conditions for the next year, year and a half, and demonstrate to the world that they are both reliable in this regard—but, as you know, Russia has not been willing, as yet, to guarantee a year-long price to Ukraine.

The CHAIRMAN. Senator Rubio.

Senator RUBIO. Thank you, Mr. Chairman.

Thank you all for being here. I know you have a difficult job.

I wanted to, Secretary Nuland, focus on a bill that has been filed in the Senate that Senator Corker's taken the lead on. It is called the Russian Aggression Prevention Act of 2014. And I was still hopeful that we can get the administration's support. Let me give you the thinking behind it. First, I am going to describe kind of how I view the situation. I would love to have your input on it.

But, it seems to me that what Putin is playing, here, is a very careful game. His ultimate goal, of course—and I do not think you would disagree with this—is, he wants to coerce Ukraine and Kiev into an agreement that guarantees Russian influence over Ukraine's foreign policy. So, they have a two-pronged plan to do this. On the one hand, they provide support for separatists. In fact,

I have seen, just in the last 48 hours, open-source reporting of evidence that they are making significant transfers again of heavy weapons to separatists in eastern Ukraine, such as tanks and armored combat vehicles. And there are signs that they intend to do more of that.

At the same time, they are also keeping alive the threat of military intervention. They have already created in their minds, the rhetorical groundwork for that sort of intervention, for humanitarian reasons that they have made up, but there are now also open-source implications that they are beginning to redeploy military units along the northeastern Ukrainian border for the first time since the May withdrawal of forces. And that includes armored vehicles, artillery, air defense units. My sense is that, given the recent offensive gains made by Kiev, the threat of military intervention will rise again.

The flip side of it is, they play this very careful game of, you know, this public role that they now have of calling for a cease-fire so they can appear like they are the mediators and Kiev is the aggressor. Up until now, they have actually, I think, quite frankly, played that game fairly well. For example, when Putin asked that the force of authorization—the use-of-force authorization be lifted, immediately thereafter, the EU Foreign Ministers decided not to impose additional sanctions. And, by the way, I think this is part of a broader strategy that they have of cutting into Western unity on the idea of new sanctions.

But, I also think—this is my guess, here, but I would be curious to your input on it—that there is probably some serious divisions in Moscow about the way forward. On the one hand, you have got these hardliners, of which Putin may be one of them, that want to see a tougher stance. And you probably have the separatists, themselves, feeling like, as much as Moscow has done, it should be more. On the other hand, you probably have a bunch of elitists in the government in Russia that worry about the broader implication of more sanctions.

One example, especially in the energy sector, is that Asia is going to soon overtake Europe as Russia's leading export market, especially after this latest deal. But, they are going to really struggle, I believe, to meet their demands and the commitments that they have made. Sanctions have made it harder for them to access foreign financing and Western technology. For example, one of the ways they choose to—they plan to meet their commitments to China is in the eastern Siberia fields that they intend to use, and—but, this field is going to be harder to develop than most others, because they have high levels of deposits of helium and so forth. It is similar to a challenge they are already facing off the coast of—I think it is the—am I pronouncing it right?—the Sakhalin Islands, where they are having—I think they are 10 years off base, in terms of doing that. And China, by the way, knows this. I would—again, I do not know, and they obviously have not shown me the deal. But, I would bet you that, in the deal that they have done with China, the Bank of China has probably reserved the right to revoke lines of credit if Russian companies cannot access credit or cannot access the technology because of broader Western sanctions.

So, if we know this is the game that they are playing, and we know this is the balance they are going through in deciding what to do next, why would we not just put in place now, through legislation, very specific consequences for what will happen if, in fact, they move forward? In essence, why do we not—instead of leaving it an open question of what might happen, via the United States if Russia moves forward with military intervention or continues to arm these separatists, why not just put specifically in writing what that will be, including specifically, as I outlined, the access to advanced United States oil and gas technologies, so that as they are having this debate in Moscow, they do not have to guess or have conjecture about what it would mean, but they will know for a fact what it would mean if they continue? And I believe this would also have an impact on China and other Asian countries who are trying to cut deals or figure out how to access more Russian energy. Why not just put that in place in writing now so that it is clear what the consequences will be for them to continue on the course they are on?

Ms. NULAND. Senator, thank you for that.

Let me say that we have been absolutely clear in our diplomat conversation, and quite specific, including at the level of the President in his conversations with President Putin, about the kinds of additional sanctions that we are considering, including in the high-technology area.

As I said before you came in, we are also working intensively with Europe on these kinds of measures, because it is not just American companies that have this technology that Russia needs, so do European companies. So, if we move in the direction of those kinds of sanctions, they will be stronger and more effective and nonpunitive, vis-a-vis our companies, if we do it together with Europe. So, it is very much on the docket, it is very much in the conversation with Russians and with the European Union, as the kind of thing that we are looking at moving forward.

Senator RUBIO. But—so, your answer has two aspects to it. The first is, if we go on our own, if we do this by ourselves, it may undermine the Western unity that we seek, in terms of other countries in the region that also have similar technologies they can provide.

Ms. NULAND. Yes. On the one hand, if we deny U.S. companies the opportunity to invest, but European companies continue to invest, then we not only have an ineffective sanction, we have——

Senator RUBIO. No, no, I understand that that is what happens.

Ms. NULAND. Right.

Senator RUBIO. It would be ineffective. But, is the concern that, if we act alone, if we just put this in legislation alone, without working with them, that it would somehow make them less likely to join us in that endeavor?

Ms. NULAND. Senator, as I have made clear to the chairman and to the ranking member, I think, as an administration, we are open to working with you on a bipartisan piece of legislation in this regard, but we need to make sure that, if we go in this direction, that whatever we put forward, we can implement, that it does not disadvantage United States companies, vis-a-vis others, that it will be effective on Russia——

Senator RUBIO. What do you mean "disadvantage U.S. companies"?

Ms. NULAND. As I said, that if we——

Senator RUBIO. Because that sounds like you are saying, "Well, we are not going to—we do not want to sell you technology, but if other people are selling you technology, then we might as well make some money on it, too."

Ms. NULAND. No. My point is that if we were to move forward with some kind of work together on bipartisan sanctions legislation, we would want to make sure that whatever we had in that bill, we could implement together with Europe and/or we would not put ourselves in the position of hurting the American economy without hurting the Russian economy.

Senator RUBIO. Well, I guess I would just close by saying that my view on it—and I hope I can convince others of this, as well—is that, when the United States is specific—if we specifically put out there, in legislation—of course it would have to be bipartisan to pass in the Senate—if we specifically make clear, "This is what will happen if you continue to do this or if you do this," then it is no longer just Secretary Kerry, you know, on the 26th of June, saying, "You should disarm separatists, or else." It is actually in place and will happen. And I think that sort of American leadership will, in fact, bring us closer to the kind of unity we seek from our allies.

So, I truly hope that this is the direction that we will head, Mr. Chairman.

The CHAIRMAN. Senator Kaine.

Senator KAINE. Thank you, Mr. Chairman.

And thank you, to the witnesses.

One of the events in 2013 that was a precipitator of the massive street protest was Yanukovych's unwillingness to sign the EU association agreements, both the political and economic agreements. We have not yet gotten into this. In March, the political association agreement, I guess, was signed. And then, in June, the economic association agreement was signed between the new Ukrainian Government and the EU, which suggests both some EU cooperation and the effect of this election in continuing the Ukrainian path toward greater associations with the EU.

What is the significance of the signing of those association agreements, both for Ukraine and what has the reaction been in Russia to those signatures after they were balked at in the end of 2013?

Ms. NULAND. Overwhelming support, needless to say, in Ukraine. It was one of the major tenets that President Poroshenko ran on and that made him a popular and overwhelming candidate. Europe has offered Ukraine, through these agreements, not only the potential for visa-free travel for all of its citizens, but also virtually tariff-free entry to—for its products to the European market and the other way. So, it is a real economic, political, and people-to-people boost. It will require a good amount of hard work to prepare implementation.

The Russians, throughout this process, expressed some concern that, because they have tariff-free trade with Ukraine now, that there would be unintended impacts on their economic situation. They pushed very hard for consultations on the implementation of the agreement. And the European Union and Ukraine have now agreed to those. And I think, tomorrow, at the level of Trade Minister, there will be trilateral discussions among the EU, Ukraine, and Russia on how to implement the agreement in a way that has least market disruption across the region and potentially might benefit Russia, as well, so that it might begin to see this in less zero-sum terms.

Senator KAINE. Right at about the same time as the June agreement was being signed with the EU, shortly thereafter, NATO met and announced that no new nations were going to be coming into NATO—Georgia, Moldova, Ukraine—anytime soon. And, in particular about Ukraine, what has the reaction been in the Ukraine to this? Was that sort of understood among all parties, that this is a time where we move toward further European integration on the economic and political front, however we kind of put NATO aside for now? Is that sort of, you know, generally understood by the Ukrainians? Or did they object to that decision?

Ms. NULAND. Senator, both in his election campaign and since, President Poroshenko has made clear that the—for his administration, the question of closer integration between Ukraine and NATO is not on the table. So, it has not been a demand of the Ukrainian side, and the alliance respects that. As you know, this has to be a matter of choice for all nations.

Senator KAINE. I want to associate myself with some of the comments made both by the chairman and Senator Rubio on, I think, the virtues of more exploration of energy- and technology-related sanctions. And I look forward to continuing those discussions.

But, it is important for us, as we weigh sanctions, and particularly if we might have to do sanctions unilaterally, if we consider doing them ahead of Europe, that that does have effects on American companies. The last time we had a hearing on this matter here, I hypothesized, naively, not knowing anything, what a potential economic effect of financial sanctions could be on United States credit card companies that—especially the big two—that govern about 90 percent of current credit card transactions in Russia. And after just blithely hypothesizing it, I got a call the next day from one of the American companies, saying that, actually, as a result of the sanctions that have been done thus far, the Russian Government is now pursuing the creation of its own credit card infrastructure and putting laws in place that will really punish and hurt the business of the two major American-based credit card companies.

And I was wondering, Assistant Secretary Glaser, if you could talk about that a little bit, because unilateral sanctions from our side do pose some significant risks if they are not done carefully.

Mr. GLASER. Well, that is absolutely correct, Mr. Senator. I would say that some of the retaliatory or countermeasures that Russia takes to protect itself from sanctions really are just examples of Russia imposing sanctions on itself.

Senator KAINE. Yes.

Mr. GLASER. It is examples of Russia pulling itself out of the international financial system, isolating itself from the international economy, which is the exact opposite of what Russia needs to be doing in order to address its fundamental economic difficulties.

That said, we are aware that the actions we take could have impact on American business and American companies, and it is something we take quite seriously. I think American businesses and American companies understand what is at stake, and they understand that it is not business as usual with respect to Russia. And they understand what we are trying to accomplish, in terms of the future of Ukraine and the future of Europe and the future of the international community. So, they understand these are important matters. And, I think, as always, we are prepared to move forward if we need to. But, again, it should go without saying, but I think it bears repeating, it is always going to be more effective, both politically, practically, and in terms of fairness to American companies, if we can move forward multilaterally, which, again, is why I think it is time well spent, and effort well spent, to try to achieve that.

Senator KAINE. Let me just make sure. Do I have my facts right on this? Because I was just hypothesizing last time. I understand that the U.S. financial sanctions have led Russia to do legal reforms that would essentially make it near impossible for Visa and MasterCard, which now cover 90 percent of credit card transactions in Russia—the effect of our sanctions has been for Russia to move forward with legal measures that will make it virtually impossible for Visa and MasterCard to operate in that country. Am I right about that?

Mr. GLASER. Well, one of the things that Russia has done as a result of this overall situation, certainly to include United States sanctions—U.S. unilateral sanctions what we have imposed—has been to move forward on ideas that, frankly, have been circulating within Russia for quite some time, in terms of a variety of measures that would require credit card companies or other types of financial entities to locate within Russia. And yes, that would create serious problems for companies like Visa and MasterCard.

Senator KAINE. I was watching the interaction between Senator Corker and Secretary Nuland on this. You know, and the Senator was asking a very appropriate question, Why is it hard to do these things? I do not think the answer is that hard. I mean, I think unilateral sanctions without the EU could have some effect on Russia, but it also has very significant effects on us. And then, if it opens up opportunities for European businesses to take the business that we are doing, then we at least have to grapple with that kind of cost-benefit equation in moving forward.

The best sanctions are ones where we are together with the EU. That does not mean we should not do unilateral sanctions, but the ones we have done already have not only affected the European economy, but they have already had a pretty significant effect on some fairly important American businesses. And we just have to balance that out.

Thank you, Mr. Chair.

The CHAIRMAN. Senator Markey.

Senator MARKEY. Thank you, Mr. Chairman. Thank you for holding this very important hearing.

Two weeks ago, I, along with some of my colleagues on this committee, sent a letter to the President, urging him to make energy security the centerpiece of our engagement with the new leadership in the Ukraine. This is urgent. And I am concerned that there are two threats that may be more powerful than Russian troops when it comes to the challenges facing the new Ukrainian Government, and they are both related to energy.

First, Russia has shut off the natural-gas spigots to Ukraine. That is half of Ukraine's supply. Gone. When winter arrives and natural-gas demand spikes, this could become a crisis.

Second, Ukraine has begun eliminating their energy subsidies. Energy subsidies provided by the Ukrainian Government are massive, amounting to 8 percent of the country's entire GDP. The $17 billion loan package approved by the IMF to stabilize the Ukrainian economy includes requirements that Ukraine gradually eliminate these subsidies. As a result, retail natural-gas rates in Ukraine will rise by 56 percent this year, another 40 percent next year, and another 20 percent in 2016 and 2017. That is a potential new source of instability. Ukraine's subsidies do make energy markets opaque, inefficient, and susceptible to corruption, but they are also extremely popular. They keep energy affordable for many households.

Now we are talking about a brand new government coming in and ushering in a doubling of energy prices. This is, of course, music to Putin's ears. He wants nothing more than a Ukrainian population distrustful of their government and looking for alternatives.

Ukraine needs an Apollo-project-like effort to become more energy efficient and increase production within their borders in order to get off of Russian gas. And, like the Apollo project, failure is not an option in this area, either. There is a narrow window of time to help this new government consolidate support and give Ukrainians a credible bulwark against Russia.

So, Ambassador, are you concerned about the reaction from middle- and low-income people in Ukraine when their energy bills skyrocket 56 percent right after the new government takes control?

Ms. NULAND. Well, Senator, thank you for your commitment to this issue in Ukraine. It is also a priority of the Ukrainian Government and it is a priority of the assistance efforts that we have going with the Ukrainians.

As you know, I think, these price hikes in energy were part of the IMF requirement for Ukraine to get healthy, which is why, when we came to the Congress to ask you for the billion dollars for the loan guarantee, we earmark, in coordination with the Ukrainian Government, the vast majority of it to help insulate the most vulnerable in the Ukrainian population from these kinds of adjustments, particularly in household energy prices. So, we have already made a huge downpayment there.

When you get our congressional notification, that I make reference to in my testimony, for the remaining $59 million we have this year for assistance, you will see a large chunk for the whole complex of energy issues, from energy efficiency to restructuring the sector, to diversification. You, yourself, have said in previous hearings, accurately, that Ukraine wastes a third of its energy out the windows and in other inefficient ways. But, we are also working aggressively with European allies and partners on reverse flow. We have had good success in beginning reverse flow gas into

Ukraine from Bulgaria, Slovakia, Hungary. We are going to continue those efforts, in coordination with the European Commission.

Senator MARKEY. Thirty-five Ukrainian mayors sent a letter urgently requesting assistance in increasing the energy efficiency of their buildings and district heating systems. We are talking about inefficient Soviet-era boilers, buildings without thermostats, uninsulated steam pipes, really the lowest of low-hanging fruit all right there, with these mayors begging for help. Are you finding an appetite within the new Ukraine to move rapidly and to have additional United States assistance to help with this project? Because, ultimately, we need to have some kind of goals that the government is establishing. And perhaps you could give us some sense of what you believe is a reasonable goal for the Ukraines to reach, in terms of increased energy efficiency, perhaps over the next 2 years, over the next 5 years, et cetera.

Ms. NULAND. Senator, we will get you the Energy Department's assessment of how quickly they can move.

But, they are making this a priority. As you know, they have to change the tax base, they have to change the incentive structure for Ukrainian industry, in particular, to reform. Interestingly, in the conversations we have had with the Ukrainian Government about the challenges of revitalizing Ukraine's east and recovering if they can bring peace and security back, one of their focuses is on energy efficiency and recapturing revenue that is lost in these rust-belt industries.

So, let me just do a shout-out to one of the requests that we have made of the Congress, which is to be able to use funding from the Western New Independent States Enterprise Fund for microprojects in the east, some of them targeted specifically at retooling old factories.

Senator MARKEY. Okay. Well, I think——

Ms. NULAND [continuing]. I would just ask you to support that.

Senator MARKEY. I think that that is an excellent request. But, I would like to see enhanced, increased attention to this area, because, obviously, with a 56-percent increase in natural-gas prices coming up this winter, and with 35 mayors writing about their old Soviet-style buildings and boilers, there is a big appetite right now to make a quick change. A quick change. And I just think that we have to front-burner this issue to help them to move very, very quickly. Because, again, that is what will keep Putin and Gazprom sleepless at night, if they do believe that they are responding to their mayors, who realize the bills, which are going to be run up.

And so, again, I urge you to have a program of that nature, and to set real goals. I think there has to be real goals that are set in this energy sector. Same thing is true, by the way, for natural gas. I think if we are going to be helping them with new technologies—and we should have a telescoped timeframe that we create, then, for a doubling of natural-gas production inside of Ukraine. And we should set those goals, set benchmarks, and then let us meet them. Because that is the real threat to Ukraine from Russia. And once we do that, I think that country will feel a lot better about its ability to be able to cope with this threat that is almost primarily energy related.

And so, I think, perhaps by the next time we have a hearing on this subject, Mr. Chairman, if we could have the concrete goals that are being set, especially for this winter, and the message that are being sent to the Ukrainian people. That will counter the propaganda that is going to come in from Putin as to the suffering that he will say is unnecessarily being inflicted by the Ukrainian Government on his own people. I just think we need a counter message that is very concrete and not vague.

I thank you, Mr. Chairman.

The CHAIRMAN. Thank you, Senator. And I appreciate your ideas. I think we will take them and try to move them forward here in the committee.

Let me just say, I appreciate the thoughtful remarks of Senator Murphy and Senator Kaine. As we close this panel, because I want to go to our second distinguished panel before the 12 o'clock vote that is coming up next, I understand that there are never simple or great choices in these matters. But, time is on Putin's side. And I say that because he certainly believes he can wait out the United States and the European Union and maintain enough instability in the Ukraine to damage its economy, to frustrate its public—such as in the context of energy, as Senator Markey just talked about— and to undermine the government's political cohesion.

In short, Putin does not have to win today. He only needs to generate a frozen conflict in eastern Ukraine that he can exploit when the world has moved on. And that has been his standard operating procedure for years—Russia has used it in Georgia and in Moldova, where Russian troops continue to occupy territory and back separatists. By giving the world the appearance of responsibility and reasonability by asking the Parliament to withdraw the law authorizing the use of military force in the Ukraine, Putin successfully gave those who wish to avoid the G7 sectoral sanctions at the end of June ammunition to argue against action at the time.

So, we have seen this movie before, and he has been successful in it. And I would just hope, as I said to Chancellor Merkel when we had the opportunity to have dinner with her—as I have said to others who have come to visit with us from the European Union, and to our own government—that if we have seen this movie before, and we know how it plays out, we should be able to not have the movie repeat itself with the same ending. And that is really my concern here. I do not see us, at this point in time, where we are headed, changing the course of events in a way that this will not play out in—nobody even talks about Crimea anymore.

Thank you all for your testimony. We will look forward to continuing to engage with you on this issue.

Let me call up our next panel. We have two very distinguished former National Security Advisors: Stephen Hadley, the former National Security Advisor to President Bush and now a principal at Rice Hadley Gates, LLC; and Zbigniew Brzezinski, counselor and trustee at the Center for Strategic and International Studies, the author of countless books, to give us the benefit of his profound insight into world history and world affairs.

We are incredibly pleased to welcome both of these gentlemen back to the committee. We look forward to your testimony.

If I could have my friends in the press—so that I can see our witnesses. Thank you.

We welcome you back to the committee. We would remind you that your full statements will be included in the record. As you can see, members have a lot of questions on these issues and would like to take advantage of your expertise, and we want to have time for that, especially since there is a 12 o'clock vote.

So, with that, Dr. Brzezinski, we will start with you, and then we will go to Mr. Hadley, and then we will get to questions.

Just push the button there, yes.

STATEMENT OF ZBIGNIEW K. BRZEZINSKI, FORMER U.S. NATIONAL SECURITY ADVISOR, COUNSELOR AND TRUSTEE, CENTER FOR STRATEGIC AND INTERNATIONAL STUDIES, WASHINGTON, DC

Dr. BRZEZINSKI. Thank you, Mr. Chairman, Senators.

Since I know your time is very limited, I do not think I am going to read to you my statement, even though it is actually fairly short. I will merely summarize the three key points that I try to make in it.

I acknowledge the fact that what Putin tried to do 3 months ago in regards to Crimea is not the same thing as he is trying to do in regards to Ukraine as a whole. Nonetheless, at the time, it generated enormous enthusiasm in Russia; and, in fact, a session of the Russian Parliament at which he presided on March 18 was really like a jamboree on the subject of chauvinism, Russia's world role, the unity of all Russian speakers around the world, and the role of Russia as a global civilization.

Since then, I think realism has begun to intrude more directly, namely that Ukraine will not fall quickly, that Ukraine is not resigned to being simply a member of a renamed version of the Soviet Union or of the tsarist empire, and that there is a rising will in Ukraine to deal with their legacies of wasted 20 years of Ukrainian independence, and that major reforms are necessary, but also acts of will designed to show Ukrainian determination to be an independent nation.

This is the context. And I think Putin has to realize by now that he has to think of alternative choices. I outline them more fully in my statement, but the first is, of course, some sort of an accommodation with the West. And I try to outline in my statement what might be the principal features of such an accommodation, one which does not meet the maximum objectives of those in the West who would like to see Ukraine a member of the European Union, but also of NATO, but it certain does not meet, also, the maximum objectives of Russia, which would like to see Ukraine subordinated to Moscow in the context of the so-called Eurasian Union. There are other specifics that would have to be considered, but that, in a sense, strikes me as a possible framework for an accommodation.

Failing that, Putin has the option of continuing more directly to destabilize Ukraine. He has done this recently. That has not worked that well. He could attempt it on a larger scale. But, if he does, I rather expect, from what one knows of the attitudes specifically of Chancellor Merkel and of President Hollande, of France, on this subject, that acts of a more overt and drastic type on the larger scale to destabilize Ukraine would precipitate the kinds of sanctions that had been planned and which the United States would like to see implemented sooner rather than later. And that remains a bone of contention in the alliance, but they are there. And the initial sanctions have sent at least ominous signals to the Russians not to take these issues lightly.

The third alternative, of course, is a complete showdown, militarily, on the model, perhaps, of Crimea, but overlooking the reality that all of Ukraine is far more complicated than a relatively small peninsula, the object of a sudden and unexpected attack. I think it is quite clear that if there were to be a larger Russian intervention, the Ukrainians would resist on a protracted basis; and especially, the risk of urban warfare for taking Ukraine over would entail the necessity of occupying the large cities—ultimately, Kiev itself—is something that no Russian leader can contemplate lightly. It could become protracted, bloody, very costly, and the result would be a disaster, both for Ukraine and for Russia. Both would be basket cases as a consequence of anything of this sort.

So, the choices that Mr. Putin has to make are not easy, but they are there, and they reflect the fact that I think it is becoming increasingly clear to him that he should not confuse a brief triumph in which he exalted, a few months ago, in Crimea, with the larger dilemma of Ukraine and the longer range relationship of Russia to the global community.

As it is—and I will end on this—Russia's international position has deteriorated. It is certainly no longer a serious partner with the United States. There are more and more questions about Russia's role in the world in Europe. And insofar as China is concerned, it is increasingly evident that, if there is any relationship between Russia and China that has any degree of depth to it, it is an asymmetrical relationship in which China, by far, is the senior partner that can insist on terms favorable to it, as was the case in the recent energy agreement with Russia. And Russia is a junior partner, geographically, culturally, and demographically, culturally and borderwise vulnerable to Chinese pressure.

So, I think that is where I will stop. The statement goes into these issues at greater length.

Thank you, Mr. Chairman, for giving me this opportunity.

[The prepared statement of Dr. Brzezinski follows:]

PREPARED STATEMENT OF DR. ZBIGNIEW BRZEZINSKI

More than 3 months have passed since Putin's triumphalist speech to the Russian Parliament. In it, he exalted in his military seizure of Crimea while basking in an orgy of unleashed chauvinistic sentiments. Putin clearly relished the enthusiasm and apparently gave little thought to the larger and longer term strategic consequences of what he unleashed.

Three months later, with continuing uncertainty regarding the future of Russo-Ukrainian relations, but also growing international costs for Russia itself, Putin faces three basic choices.

(1) To accommodate with Ukraine by terminating the assault on Ukrainian sovereignty and economic well-being. This will not be easy to do, and it will require wisdom and persistence both from Russia as well as Ukraine and the West. Essentially, an accommodation should involve the termination of the Russian efforts to destabilize Ukraine from within, not to mention ending possible threats of a larger military invasion—as well as some sort of an East-West understanding which entails Russia's tacit acceptance of Ukraine's prolonged journey toward eventual EU membership. At the same time, it should be made clear to all concerned that

Ukraine neither seeks nor the West contemplates Ukrainian membership in the NATO alliance. It is reasonable for the Russians to feel uncomfortable about that prospect.

At the same time, it would be made clear that Russia no longer expects Ukraine to become part of the "Eurasian Union," a designation which is a transparent cover for the recreation of something approximating the former Soviet Union or the Tsarist Empire. An understanding regarding this issue should not preclude, however, a Russian-Ukrainian trade deal, based on the fact that from a purely economic point of view, both countries can benefit from normal and increasingly cooperative trade as well as financial relations.

The international community, specifically the West, could in some fashion reiterate their support for that outcome, not to mention the full scale resumption of more normal relations with Russia itself, including the lifting of existing sanctions.

(2) Putin's second choice is to continue the effort to destabilize Ukraine by sponsoring thinly veiled military intervention designed to disrupt normal life in portions of Ukraine. Should Russia continue on this course, obviously the West would have to undertake a full scale, prolonged, and truly painful application of sanctions designed to convey to Russia the painful consequences of its unwarranted violation of Ukraine's sovereignty. In effect, this very unfortunate outcome would likely produce the emergence of two basket cases in Eastern Europe: in Ukraine because of deliberate Russian actions; and in Russia itself as a justified consequence of the needed Western reaction to its aggression.

(3) Putin's third choice could involve the decision to invade Ukraine across the board, exploiting Russia's obviously much larger military potential. Such an action, however, would not only prompt sustained retaliation by the West but could provoke prolonged Ukrainian resistance, especially based on spontaneous outbursts of anger in its larger cities. In these conditions, it is unlikely that the West would remain entirely passive. If the resistance was sustained and intense, there would be growing pressure on the members of NATO to provide various forms of support for the Ukrainians, thereby making the conflict much more prolonged and costly to the aggressor.

For the Kremlin, the consequence of the third option would be not only a permanently hostile Ukrainian population of more than 40 million people, but also an economically retarded and politically isolated Russia, facing the growing possibility of increasing internal unrest.

In brief, the obvious choice for everyone concerned is to find a formula for international accommodation, and that has to involve the abandonment of the use of force against Ukraine by Russia. The issue of Crimea will remain unresolved for the time being, but it will be an enduring reminder that chauvinistic fanaticism is not the best point of departure for the resolution of larger and more complex issues. This is why Putin's actions are a threat not only to the West but ultimately also to Russia itself.

The CHAIRMAN. Thank you, Dr. Brzezinski.
Mr. Hadley.

STATEMENT OF HON. STEPHEN J. HADLEY, FORMER U.S. NATIONAL SECURITY ADVISOR, PRINCIPAL, RICE HADLEY GATES, LLC, WASHINGTON, DC

Mr. HADLEY. Thank you very much for the opportunity to be with you this morning.

I have a statement, which I have submitted, that talks about what Putin is up to, how far he is likely to press his current actions, what should be our objectives and strategy for dealing with it. I will just leave that for the record.

The bottom line I try to make is that we have seen in the past that Putin's objectives escalate as he succeeds and is not met with resistance or counter pressure. And therefore, I think it is important that we be putting together the elements of a strategy that will put on that counter pressure.

I thought what I might do with my time is try to answer some of the questions that you have raised in the first session, and give you my answers to them, for what it is worth.

Why is the administration so——

The CHAIRMAN. Mr. Hadley, could you just take that microphone and put it closer to you?

Mr. HADLEY. Yes, sir, sorry.

The CHAIRMAN. There we go, perfect. Thank you.

Mr. HADLEY. So, why is the—thank you, Mr. Chairman—why is the administration reluctant on sanctions? I think it is partly, one, they want to have unity with the Europeans, because they do not want to let Putin drive a wedge between the United States and Europe. And I think that is right.

Second, I think it is an effectiveness point. If you look at foreign direct investment, 75 percent of foreign direct investment in Russia comes from the EU. The United States only has about $10 billion a year. We are 10th, in terms of foreign investment. If you look at trading relations, we are the 12th export partner, the 5th import partner of Russia. So, we do not have the economic clout. And if you really want to be effective, you want to have the Europeans along, because that is where the investment and the trading relations are.

Third, I think they are reluctant because sometimes sanctions are more effective in the anticipation than they are in the execution.

So, I think that explains the reluctance.

I think, though, as I say in the statement, we have telegraphed this punch so often without delivering it, I think it raises a question of credibility. And therefore, I think, Mr. Chairman, in response to your point, if the Europeans do not act on July 16, I think we are going to be forced to go ahead unilaterally. But, I would hope we would do it in the following way: having worked with Chancellor Merkel, who has the lead on this within Europe, with an understanding that we will go first and she will do her best so that the Europeans will follow.

Similarly, the legislation, Senator Rubio, that you talked about that Senator Corker, I think, is sponsoring, a kind of a roadmap of what will happen if Putin persists in this activity, I think that can be a very useful tool, but I would hope it would not only have bipartisan support within the Congress, but is something we would have worked with the Europeans so that it, in fact, becomes a roadmap for what we and the Europeans will do together if Russia and Putin persist. That does not mean that it has to be unilaterally—has to be multilateral at the time it is adopted. It—what we would hope is—many times, we have to lead the Europeans by taking action, but with an understanding that, hopefully, in the end of the day, we will end up on the same page.

Last two points and one I think—I saw Dr. Brzezinski's article in the Post this morning, and I thought it was a very good statement. I only have one small quibble with it, which answers one of the questions Senator Kaine asked. We ought to be strengthening Ukraine's capacity to defend itself, and other states that are at risk from pressure from Russia. The issue of NATO enlargement is not on the table. The Ukrainians have not asked. For them to join NATO would be a long process, years in the future. So, it is not on the table. But, I would also not explicitly take it off the table and say that the door is closed to Ukraine, because I would not like to reward Putin for his pressure. And I think we need to stick to the principle that countries should be free to select the alliances they choose, free of coercion, pressure, or the use of force.

Finally, last point—as I say in my statement, I think there are elements of policy that we need to put in place that are probably even more important than sanctions. And sanctions over the long term, I think, we want to do in a way that does not close the door on Russia, does not say to Ukraine that, "If you come West, you have to sever your historical and economic ties with Russia." I do not think that is smart. I think we need to leave the door open for a Russia that will change its policies and come back to the post-cold-war consensus and want to move West. And I think we should do that to keep faith with those people in Russia that hope for a more democratic and a more Western-oriented future for their country.

Thank you very much, Mr. Chairman.

[The prepared statement of Mr. Hadley follows:]

PREPARED STATEMENT OF STEPHEN J. HADLEY

RUSSIA AND ONGOING DEVELOPMENTS IN UKRAINE

It is a great privilege to have the opportunity to appear before the committee this morning. I would like to discuss briefly what Russian President Putin is seeking to achieve by his actions in Ukraine, how far he is likely to press these actions, what should be U.S. and allied objectives in dealing with the Russian challenge in Ukraine, and what would be the elements of a strategy to achieve these objectives. The views I will express are my own and not the views of any organization with which I may be affiliated.

What is President Putin Seeking To Achieve By His Actions in Ukraine?

President Putin is often quoted as saying that one of the greatest tragedies of the 20th century was the dissolution of the Soviet Union. He gives as a principal reason for this conclusion the fact that it left hundreds of thousands of ethnic Russians and Russian-speakers outside the borders of Mother Russia. For two decades he has said his interests were in better treatment of Russian nationals living as ethnic minorities in countries outside Russia. But when he ordered the invasion of Georgia in 2008, the invasion and annexation of Crimea in 2014, and the active subversion and destabilization of eastern Ukraine, President Putin went way beyond any reasonable action aimed at improving the situation of these minorities. Instead President Putin has attacked, violated, and repudiated the basic principles of the post-cold-war settlement in Europe: acceptance of existing borders, respect for the sovereignty and territorial integrity of all states, and the right of all states to choose their affiliations and alliances free of coercion and the threat or use of force.

President Putin has an alternative vision for Europe that is less the recreation of the Soviet Union than the restoration of Russian greatness. Through the Eurasian Union, the Eurasian Customs Union, and the Collective Security Treaty Organization, President Putin hopes to establish a Russian-dominated confederation of states between the European Union on the one hand and China and the Asian States on the other. With Belarus, Kazakhstan, and Russia as core members, and Armenia, Kyrgyzstan, and Tajikistan likely additions, he is off to a good start. But he needs Ukraine to give the organization real economic and geopolitical heft. That means he must prevent Ukraine from becoming part of the economic and security organizations to its West, namely the European Union (EU) and the North Atlantic Treaty Organization (NATO). And that is what his efforts in Ukraine—as well as Georgia—have been about.

How Far is President Putin Likely To Press These Actions?

During the crisis provoked by President Putin's invasion of Georgia, his initial objectives were somewhat limited. But as the operation succeeded, and when he thought his actions might not be effectively opposed, his objectives expanded accordingly. Indeed, he ultimately embraced the objective of toppling the democratically elected Georgian Government in Tbilisi. Efforts by the United States and its allies, among other factors, caused the Russians ultimately to stop short of this objective.

Similar "objective escalation" occurred in the wake of his "success" in Crimea and could expand in connection with Russian action in eastern Ukraine or elsewhere.

One concern would be if Russia's active subversion and destabilization campaign were to succeed in Ukraine, President Putin might try something similar in one or more of the Baltic States, such as Latvia. The objective here would be to show that the article 5 security guarantee given to these countries as NATO members was not worth the paper it is written on and could not protect these countries from being destabilized and perhaps even losing part of their territory.

At the most extreme end of the "objective escalation" spectrum, President Putin might even seek to split or destabilize the European Union itself. We know that he has been cultivating relations with extremist political parties in Europe particularly on the political right. These extremist parties have mostly only one thing in common—they oppose the European Union. Destabilizing the European Union could be attractive in its own right. But it could also preoccupy the EU with its own internal survival so as to distract it from efforts to reach out and embrace Ukraine, Moldova, Georgia, and other countries between the European Union and Russia's Eurasian Union.

The best way to seek to prevent President Putin from moving up the "objective escalation" ladder is to seek to deny him success in his current efforts and to show that any future efforts will be effectively opposed.

What Should Be U.S. and Allied Objectives In Dealing With the Russian Challenge in Ukraine?

The United States should work with its friends and allies to seek to:

- Deter Russia from further action against Ukraine or any other state—in violation of the basic principles of the post-cold-war settlement in Europe.
- Deny targets of opportunity that President Putin can exploit to advance his agenda or, to put it another way, either eliminate or harden Europe's vulnerabilities against further Russian action.
- Reassure those NATO allies vulnerable to Russian pressure of NATO's article 5 commitment to their security.
- Reenergize the historic vision that the United States and its friends and allies share of a Europe whole, free, and at peace as an alternative to President Putin's vision of Russian domination of its neighbors and of increasing authoritarianism at home.
- Distinguish between Putin and Russia and thereby avoid re-dividing Europe or seeking to exclude or isolate Russia from Europe by disregarding or disrupting the historical and economic ties between Russia and its neighbors to the West.

I understand that this last point will be controversial in some quarters given the total unacceptability of President Putin's actions. But it is in the interest of the United States and the rest of Europe to keep the door open to Russia to take its place in a Europe based on the post-cold-war principles on which a Europe whole, free, and at peace can be built. This will require Russia to change its current behavior, either because of a change of heart on the part of President Putin (however unlikely) or because of the efforts of those in Russia committed to a more democratic and peaceful future for their country. We must leave the door open to them—to give them hope.

What Would Be the Elements of a Strategy To Achieve These Objectives?

Briefly, a comprehensive strategy seeking to achieve these objectives could include the following elements:

- Complete the Transatlantic Trade and Investment Partnership (TTIP) as a way to bind Europe together and to the United States in a relationship of economic growth and prosperity—extending the agreement to include those European countries with customs unions or free trade agreements with the EU already, such as Ukraine and Turkey, while leaving the door open for, ultimately, a more peaceful and democratic Russia.
- Develop a joint transatlantic energy strategy that will reduce the EU's dependence on Russian oil and gas—through such things as liquid natural gas (LNG) shipments from the United States, the development of shale oil and shale gas in Europe, better use of existing pipeline infrastructure to reduce dependence on Russia, and construction of new non-Russian controlled pipelines.
- Resume the European Union's "open door" to association agreements and ultimately membership for those countries to its east that seek such membership—and include them in a way that does not require them to sever existing and historical economic ties to Russia.

- Recommit the United States to the security of Europe in both word and deed, through additional deployments and exercises of American forces in Europe along with our NATO allies and other friends.
- Revitalize the NATO alliance by additional planning, exercises, and military capability—especially on the part of America's NATO allies—directed to NATO's core mission of maintaining security in Europe—while maintaining an open door to new members that meet its criteria.
- Help nations subject to Russian pressure to strengthen their own capacity to defend their territory from either armed attack or subversion/destabilization including by providing military, paramilitary, and police training and equipment.
- Help the Ukrainian people to overcome two decades of squandered trust and missed opportunity by their leaders and to build an inclusive, democratic, and noncorrupt government and market-based economy that can provide security and prosperity to all Ukrainians.

There has been a lot of talk about economic sanctions against Russia. These are an important element of a comprehensive strategy. So far, the United States and its allies have threatened more sanctions then they have delivered, undercutting the credibility of this element of strategy. But sanctions are only part of a strategy not the sum total of it. The level of the sanctions imposed on Russia in the short term should not be the measure of the success or failure of the overall strategy. For the goal of the strategy should be to change over time what might be called the "correlation of forces" in Europe so as to reduce Russia's leverage and deter the kind of Russian actions we have seen in Georgia and Ukraine. In this context, the other elements of a comprehensive strategy outlined above are perhaps as important if not more important than short-term economic sanctions.

The CHAIRMAN. Well, thank you both. It takes tremendous talent to be able to synthesize major concepts in such a short period of time. And I have read the testimony, and it is very instructive.

My concern—I always prefer multilateral sanctions, when we can get them. I prefer not to have sanctions if we do not even need them in order to achieve our goals. If diplomatic discourse can ultimately lead us to a point where we can negotiate an agreement that is acceptable, obviously that is desirable as well. But, looking at Russia's history here, with Georgia, Moldova, and now the Ukraine, at some point—and I think you may have alluded to this by saying we may have to go first—at some point, if there is to be no significant arming of the Ukrainian military so that the challenges of the Russians trying to take them on are further exacerbated—Dr. Brzezinski has already said the Ukrainians will fight tooth-and-nail, especially in urban centers, and that that would be a concept that no Russian leader could fathom doing. But this would enhance that possibility.

Also, if we are not to, at the end of the day, pursue any sanctions because the Europeans are unwilling to, what is to stop Putin from continuing on a course of destabilization? Not invasion, but destabilization. And what is it that sends him a message that the next place that he picks, he is free to do so, because, at the end of the day, he will get condemnation, but no other consequences?

Either one of you, I am happy to——

Dr. BRZEZINSKI. Well, Mr. Chairman, let me just——

The CHAIRMAN. If you would put your button on; your microphone.

Dr. BRZEZINSKI. Let me briefly make one comment on your observation of guarding the NATO issue. I think there is a misunderstanding here. I make it very clear that NATO membership can be forsaken. The Ukrainians are not asking for it. A large proportion of the Ukrainian people do not want to be in it. And, in any case, if it were to transpire that there is an accommodation, I think, in that context, it would be possible to negotiate it with the Ukrainians not being promised or having door open for them in the future regarding NATO. One can, I think, understand the Russian concerns here if one look at the map. NATO membership would jut a large, large new area deep into what traditionally has been the Russian Empire and create an altogether new geopolitical situation, which I cannot see the Russians ever accepting unless there is a significant accommodation of—larger sense. And that is all I had in mind.

On the question of the arms, my view is that we should be very open about it, and not secretive. If the Ukrainians need arms for their defense, we should be willing to provide them, although in a manner which does not provide for a capacity of the Ukrainians to undertake offensive actions. The Russians would exploit any transfer of arms to the Ukrainians as a threat to their security. If we are very deliberate, in terms of what we convey to the Ukrainians, we can enhance their capacity, particularly to defend their cities, and make the attempt to occupy any large cities by the Russian Armed Forces prohibitively expensive. And that will have, then, political consequences of a prolonged conflict, financial consequences internationally, mobilization of public opinion internationally against Russia, which I think would make any rational Russian Government think twice of that option.

Mr. HADLEY. Mr. Chairman, I think sanctions are an important element of a comprehensive policy, and at some point we may have to go out ahead to lead by example as a way to bring the Europeans along. But, I think we must focus equally on the other elements of a comprehensive strategy that, over the long term, are going to be more important in reducing Putin's leverage and his ability to pursue these kinds of activities. Completing the TTIP negotiations has been talked about; developing a joint transatlantic energy strategy that reduces the EU's dependence on Russian oil and gas; resuming an open door to accession to the European Union; the United States recommitting to the security of Europe, in word and deed, by some of our deployments and exercises; revitalizing the NATO alliance; getting Europeans to make more of a commitment and to refocus on the core mission of preserving and protecting the security of Europe; helping the nations that are subject to Russian pressure to build self-defense forces; and finally, helping Ukraine succeed as a democratic, prosperous country able to provide security and prosperity for its people. Those long-term commitments are what are really going to eliminate the opportunities for Putin to make mischief in the future.

The CHAIRMAN. I appreciate that.

Let me ask one last question. From the end of the cold war, attempts have been made to draw Russia into the community of nations as a stable, prosperous, and democratic partner. But, given Putin's high level of domestic support in recent polls, I guess there is some allure, among Russians, of the empire or power over other countries as being attractive. Could we have done things differently that would have changed the course of events, or was Putin's Russia inevitable? And what kind of policies would you advocate—and you were referring to keeping the door open, Mr. Hadley—that the United States and international community should follow to encourage Russia to forsake imperial aspirations and to get back into an international order, which they have upended by virtue of their invasion in Crimea and what they are doing in the Ukraine?

These questions are for both of you. I would like to hear from both of you on this.

Dr. BRZEZINSKI. Basically, I think we have to maintain the policy that we have adopted in the wake of the collapse of the Soviet Union, which is to create opportunities for Russia's closer association with the West, but without compromising our fundamental principles and while entertaining the hope that, over time, internal change in Russia will contribute to the gradual democratization of Russia itself.

There is some evidence to indicate that this, in the longer run, is not only possible, but even probable. There is developing a Russian middle class which increasingly thrives on essentially adopting as much as possible of the Western lifestyle and of connectivity with the West. It sends the children to the West. It travels to the West. It sends its money to the West. And perhaps that is most persuasive of all.

Basically, a process is taking place which is demonstrated by the scale of the social opposition, the demonstrations, the increasing number of commentators speaking up openly on this issue. And that is part of a process of change which one can cultivate.

Putin's current moves are, in my judgment, a retrogressive aberration connected very much with his personality, his previous institutional connections, in particular with the instruments of compulsion, perhaps a certain touch of megalomania on a personal level. And he appeals on that basis to those elements of Russian society which feel themselves vulnerable, which are very nationalistic, which are susceptible to chauvinistic appeals. And we saw exactly that manifesting itself in the wake of the seemingly very easy so-called, "triumph" in Crimea.

But, the crisis with Ukraine, I think, is beginning to send signals, particularly to the more intelligent internationally minded parts of the Russian elite, that Russia is being drawn into something that could prove utterly debilitating to Russia itself. And this is why, in the longer run, I anticipate that there will be some inclination to experiment, to check out, to investigate the possibility of some sort of an accommodation once it dawns, not only on the Russian elite itself, but increasingly maybe on Mr. Putin himself, that the policy of violence, either selective or all-out, is, in the long run, not the road to success, but a guarantee of Russia as a basket case economically and politically.

The CHAIRMAN. Mr. Hadley.

Mr. HADLEY. I agree very much with what Dr. Brzezinski has said. Putin views himself as a strong leader who wants to return to Russian greatness, but he has a definition of Russian greatness, I would say, that is 19th century, it is sort of a new neo-Russian Empire. We have to show him that, whatever his short-term tactical successes, his actions involve a long-term strategic loss and the real future for Russia as a secure and prosperous state is going to be, not on 19th-century principles, but on 21st-century principles. And those—and we need to, therefore, deter him from his 19th-century agenda and leave the door open for those who want

Russia to actually have a 21st-century role of—as—and path for a secure and prosperous state.

The CHAIRMAN. Thank you both.

Senator Corker.

Senator CORKER. Thank you, Mr. Chairman.

And thank you both for being here. We always appreciate having distinguished National Security Advisors here, and appreciate your comments.

And, Dr. Brzezinski, when you say "accommodation," in answering the last question, an accommodation to Russia once the thinking of the elites permeates the rest of society or Putin, what kind of accommodation would that be?

Dr. BRZEZINSKI. Well, are we talking specifically, in your question, about Ukraine, or more generally?

Senator CORKER. Specifically relative to Ukraine.

Dr. BRZEZINSKI. Well, it seems to me that increasingly it is a fact, and no longer a speculation, that Ukraine, as an independent state, is going to be moving toward the West. That is the predominant predisposition of the Ukrainian people. I think the regime that has now emerged in Ukraine is generally democratic. It is determined to correct the errors of the last 20 years. For, I am sad to say, over the last 20 years, Ukraine has been governed very badly.

Senator CORKER. Right.

Dr. BRZEZINSKI. And I think that it is evident to all concerned that the regimes that have dominated the political scene were self-serving, self-enriching, and not dedicated to Ukraine's well-being. This is now changing, in part, to the challenge from the outside. The use of force against Ukraine by the Russians was a stunning experience for the Ukrainians. Historically, they have not been anti-Russian. But also, over the last 20 years, they have started to enjoy the fruits of independence. And that is especially the case with the younger generation. And that younger generation asserted itself in the Maidan. And I think that increasingly defines Ukraine today.

So, the Russians will have to come to terms with that new reality. But, otherwise, they will embroil themselves in a prolonged adventure, which, as I have tried to stress, would be self-debilitating.

So, I am, on the whole, an optimist. I believe an accommodation is possible, because the costs of imposing a unilateral solution by the Russians themselves are simply disproportionately high to the benefits that could be achieved thereby.

They are beginning to learn this already in the case of Crimea. There was this exaltation when they occupied Crimea—liberation, reunification, all sorts of slogans. What is the reality 3 months later? Prices have risen three times. Tourists are not coming. They come every year, on a scale of 6 million, including a great many from abroad. They are not showing up. They have difficulty even in getting there.

Investments in Ukraine are very difficult to make the moment they involve any international deal, because the international community has not recognized the incorporation of Crimea, which means there will be endless legal suits connected with any kind of development in Ukraine—tourism, exploration for more energy, or whatever.

In brief, what seemed like a great success 3 months ago is now becoming, I think, increasingly a source of concern. And this is where I sort of feel more confident about what is happening. I am frustrated that we have not adopted the sanctions that we should. I would like to see the Europeans act more decisively. I think we could, too. But, by and large, we are pointed in the right direction, and I think it is becoming more clear to more Russians that Putin is pointed in the wrong direction.

Senator CORKER. If I could—I know Hadley has to leave here soon, and I know Rubio wants to ask some questions—I will just ask one more.

One of the things that was most poignant to me on a recent trip was a comment I referred to in my opening comments, and that was a National Security Advisor in eastern Europe referring to the fact that if we allow Russia to continue with this bad behavior without the sanctions that I think both of you have alluded to, we, in essence, will accommodate a bitter peace. In other words, we return to business as usual. Nothing is really done about what has happened in Crimea and other places. Just since both of you have to think for the long haul, and have done that within differing administrations, what are the risks there, from your perspective, over the longer haul? And that is a bitter peace with Russia, where their actions have never been countered, where they just kind of fester, if you will, in Eastern Europe.

Mr. HADLEY. You know, I think one of the things that we are tripping over is the word ''accommodation,'' which suggests giving in to Russia. I would rather talk in terms of outcomes. I think it is very important that Russia be seen as not to be able to succeed with what it is doing and, as I say, that Putin sees that, and the Russian people see that, that this 19th-century nationalistic binge he has been on is not working for them. The outcome I think we want is, you know, a Ukraine, that if it decides to move West, join the EU and Western institutions, is able to do so, an outcome where Ukraine is prosperous and secure, an outcome where the Russian people within Ukraine can enjoy that security and prosperity, in which the Russians see that it is a Ukraine that is not against Russia, but is allowed to maintain its historical economic and historical ties with Russia.

And I think that if that happens, the Russian people, at some point, are going to decide that maybe Ukraine is a better model for their future than this kind of nationalistic, neo-Russian Empire that Putin is talking about. That is the outcome I think we ought to be striving for here.

Senator CORKER. Thank you both for being here.

Thank you, Mr. Chairman.

The CHAIRMAN. Senator Rubio.

Senator RUBIO. Thank you, Mr. Chairman.

Thank you both for being here. Thank you both for your service to our country over an extended period of time, both in government and outside. I appreciate your presence very much.

Dr. Brzezinski, of course, your service to our country is well documented, although these days you are increasingly known as Mika's dad. [Laughter.]

And we watch you quite often in the morning.

I wanted to ask you both, first, in the previous panel—and I know it was kind of simplistic in the way I described it, and I do not think it is inconsistent with anything you were saying, but—in my mind, the—kind of the 5,000-foot view of what Putin is trying to pull off, here, is to reach a point where he has exorbitant influence over Kiev's foreign policy, vis-a-vis his relationship to Russia. It is what we have all been talking about. And, as I have described earlier, I think that involves the combination of support for separatists and the threat of military engagement, on the one hand, and then these sort of things he is doing—calling for cease-fires and so forth—to make himself appear as the reasonable conciliator in the—juxtaposed against an image he is trying to create, that Kiev is the aggressor, and so forth.

And then I said that I thought—and this is where I hope your insight will be helpful—that, within Moscow now, within the people making these decisions, I would venture to guess—obviously, I do not know, but I would venture to guess, and I am pretty certain, that they, themselves, are kind of looking at this dynamic, and there is two opposing schools of thought. One group probably is pushing very hard for more aggressive action, and another group is probably saying, ''You know, but these sanctions are going to hurt our pocketbook and our ability to do things.'' I mean, we should not underestimate how important the Asian markets are going to be for Russia's future short-term, quite frankly, ability to export energy. And, in fact, the estimates are that Asia will become its leading export market. To do that, they have got to have the capacity. Means they have got to go and explore. I pointed to the fact that they are going to struggle in eastern Siberia, because some of these gas deposits there have high amounts of helium, and that requires extensive work. And so, they need access, not just to financing, but some of the Western technology.

What it leads me to is—as we view this dynamic, they are having this debate in Moscow about, ''We are worried about sanctions, but we also have this group that is pushing for more''—and, by the way, I would guess that, despite all the assistance they are getting, some of these separatists probably feel like Moscow is not doing enough; they want them to do more.

So, given all these pressures, it is my view that the best way to nudge it, or to influence this in the direction we would like to see it head, is not simply to threaten sanctions, but to make very clear what those sanctions would look like so that it is not a guessing game about what will happen if they do this; that, in fact, they know for a fact what it would look like. And I know that the ideal scenario is that if we do it, others will join us in it. But, my sense of it is that, potentially, the best way to ensure that is through American leadership, that if America is willing to—at least the American Congress is willing to graphically spell out what the specific consequences will be of specific actions—automatically, not what the President may decide to do—that it would strengthen our hand in that regard. And I think, Mr. Hadley, in your testimony, you said we may be getting closer to that point anyway.

So, that was the question I asked of Secretary Nuland, and I was hoping that you would both expand.

And then, if time permits, I just had an issue related to Russia, but not directly to Ukraine. And it may seem like it is out of left field, but I am curious, given the amount of knowledge that you both have about Russia, What do you think their response would be, given events in Iraq that have happened recently, if the Syrians asked the Russians to conduct airstrikes in Syria against ISIL? How open would they be to that sort of measure?

And that is a separate question if we have time to get to them. But, I really want to focus on this question of whether specific sanctions by Congress would further the direction of decision-making in Moscow.

Mr. HADLEY. I would make three points. One, I think your description of his strategy is accurate, and it is very, very important that it be seen to fail. Because if it succeeds, he will do it again elsewhere. You know, when he went into Georgia in 2008, we all said, ''Today Georgia, tomorrow Crimea, and the day after, the Baltics.'' Well, you know, he is two-thirds of the way there. So, one, it is important he fail.

Two, I think it would be very useful, as I said in my opening comments, to have that kind of roadmap, ''If he takes these activities, or fails to stop what he is doing, these are the kind of sanctions he would face.'' I think that would be a useful thing.

I would hope, though, we—as much as possible—we could coordinate it with the Europeans so that Angela Merkel would be leading the Europeans so they would follow our roadmap. That does not say we do not do it without them, but it will be more effective if we can bring them along.

Third——

Senator RUBIO. Well, they are probably in a good mood in Germany after last night's game. So, we should jump on that.

Mr. HADLEY Yes, and they may be even better after the finals.

Third, I will go back to what I said before, this is not only about sanctions. But, if we are going to be effective against Putin's strategy, we need the other six or seven items that I outlined in my statement, that are elements of a comprehensive, long-term approach to this problem. That is what we need. So, sanctions, yes; but, take a look at the other things, and let us be moving out on the other elements of a comprehensive policy.

Dr. BRZEZINSKI. I agree very much with Mr. Hadley.

Senator RUBIO. What is your view on, if the Syrians asked the Russians to conduct airstrikes against ISIL in Syria, whether they would do that?

Dr. BRZEZINSKI. Well, the first question that would come to my mind immediately is, Where would they stage it from? You know, they do not have the sea-born capability for air operations that we have. So, it would have to be done in some fashion from Russian territory.

Senator RUBIO. Or from Syrian territory that the Syrians——

Dr. BRZEZINSKI. Or—well, what facilities are really available for them on Syrian territory?

Senator RUBIO. Other than the seaport, that—the naval facility.

Dr. BRZEZINSKI. They would have to be secure, and they are probably very vulnerable, and they are probably not in very good shape.

Now, would they be tempted to do it? I rather suspect not. I think the Russians want to avoid an entanglement with the whole host of issues that are being unleashed in the Middle East, and they much prefer us to become more entangled. And this is one of the reasons why I have been urging restraint in our part, because it seems to me that these are issues that are not likely to be solved entirely by the use of force. And certainly, we have already learned from both Afghanistan and Iraq, that the use of force in these very complex ethnic, religious, national circumstances is a very, very costly and unpredictable undertaking.

Mr. HADLEY. It is a murky area, and press reports say that Russian SU–22s, I think, are flying strikes in Iraq. That is press reports. And it is unclear, are they flown by Iraqi pilots, by Russian pilots, or Iranian pilots? This is a murky and confused situation.

The CHAIRMAN. Well, thank you both for your insights and your expertise. It is always a tremendous value to the committee.

This hearing will remain open until the close of business on Friday.

And, with the thanks of the committee, this hearing is adjourned.

[Whereupon, at 11:55 a.m., the hearing was adjourned.]

ADDITIONAL MATERIAL SUBMITTED FOR THE RECORD

RESPONSE OF VICTORIA NULAND TO QUESTION SUBMITTED BY SENATOR RON JOHNSON

Question. Investment bank Credit Suisse released its "Global Wealth Report 2013" October 9 that showed 35 percent of all wealth in Russia was controlled by 110 people. The amount is equivalent to $420 billion, according to the bank. By contrast, billionaires around the world control between 1 percent and 2 percent of total wealth. The full report can be found here: http://www.scribd.com/doc/174860081/Global-Wealth-Report-2013.

◆ Are we prepared to sanction all 110 of these individuals? Which, if any, of these 110 people have already been sanctioned? Of these individuals, who will be added and specifically when? Why have we not immediately added all 110 people?

Answer. In response to Russia's ongoing violations of Ukrainian sovereignty and territorial integrity, the United States has imposed targeted sanctions on Russian individuals and entities, as well as a set of carefully calibrated sanctions on Russia's financial, energy, and defense sectors that the President announced on July 16. Since the start of the Ukraine crisis, the U.S. has sanctioned 57 individuals (18 Ukrainians, 39 Russians), six Russian banks, 14 other crony-related entities, eight defense firms, two Russian energy companies, separatist groups in Donetsk and Luhansk, and two Crimea-based energy companies under Executive Orders 13660, 13661, and 13662. Designated Russian individuals include high-ranking government officials, business executives, and members of the Russian leadership's inner circle. Broader sectoral sanctions may be deployed if Russia fails to stop destabilizing Ukraine.

The President's Executive orders with regard to the situation in Ukraine do not, however, direct that sanctions determinations be made based on an individual's net worth. Though our sanctions have targeted some of the wealthiest Russian citizens, an individual's net worth is not an independent basis for a sanctions designation under Executive Orders 13660, 13661, and 13662.

The United States and our international partners continue to press Russia to end all support to separatists in Ukraine, control the border, call on separatists to lay down their arms, return the border checkpoints, and release all remaining hostages. Until Russia takes these actions, the United States and our partners remain prepared to impose additional, tougher sanctions.

[EDITOR'S NOTE.—A copy of the full report mentioned above was too voluminous to include in the printed hearing. It will be retained in the permanent record of the committee.]